First published in 2025 by Aurum Press,
an imprint of The Quarto Group.
One Triptych Place, London, SE1 9SH,
United Kingdom
T (0)20 7700 9000
www.Quarto.com

EEA Representation, WTS Tax d.o.o., Žanova ulica 3,
4000 Kranj, Slovenia www.wts-tax.si

Text and illustration copyright © *The Spectator* 2025
Design copyright © Quarto Publishing plc 2025

The right of *The Spectator* to be identified as the author of this Work has been asserted by them in accordance with the Copyright, Designs & Patents Act 1988.

All rights reserved. No part of this book may be reproduced or utilised in any form or by any means, electronic or mechanical, including photocopying, recording or by any information storage and retrieval system, without permission in writing from Aurum Press.

A catalogue record for this book is available from the British Library.

ISBN 978-1-80570-205-4
Ebook ISBN 978-1-80570-206-1
10 9 8 7 6 5 4 3 2 1

Typeset by Typo•glyphix
Design Ben Ruocco
Illustration Martin Hargreaves
Cover design Patrick Carpenter

Printed in Pontian, Johor, Malaysia PC072025

THE SPECTATOR

Best *of*
Notes on...

From kippers to jeans
and everything in between

Edited by
William Moore and *Gus Carter*

Illustrations by *Michael Heath*

Aurum

Contents

Introduction	6

Notes on... Canapés Ysenda Maxtone Graham	8
Notes on... Jeans William Moore	10
Notes on... Carps Jon Day	12
Notes on... Land Rovers Ben Fogle	13
Notes on... Big Ben Mark Mason	14
Notes on... Mothing Mark Solomons	16
Notes on... Croquet Sam Leith	17
Notes on... Invitations Philip Womack	18
Notes on... Obituaries Mark Mason	20
Notes on... Corkscrews Henry Jeffreys	22
Notes on... Routemasters Paul Burke	24
Notes on... Gins in tins Flora Watkins	26
Notes on... Falconry Mark Cocker	28
Notes on... Trainers Justin Marozzi	30
Notes on... Kippers Andrew Watts	32
Notes on... Wassailing Matthew Dennison	34
Notes on... Foie gras Paul Levy	36
Notes on... Ordnance Survey maps Mark Mason	38
Notes on... The coronation spoon Robert Tombs	39
Notes on... Easter lilies Lara Prendergast	40
Notes on... Toffee apples Tanya Gold	42
Notes on... Cocaine Julie Burchill	44
Notes on... Standing ovations Laura Freeman	46
Notes on... Rats Jon Day	48
Notes on... Tabletop games Gus Carter	50
Notes on... Confetti Melanie McDonagh	51
Notes on... Pebble-spotting Laura Freeman	52
Notes on... Gilets Henry Jeffreys	54
Notes on... Valentine's Day Freddy Gray	56
Notes on... Elderflower Flora Watkins	58
Notes on... Bagpipes Robert Porter	60
Notes on... Viking words Frederick Edward	62
Notes on... Bowls Michael Simmons	63
Notes on... The English seaside Jenny Coad	64
Notes on... Monopoly Andrew Watts	65
Notes on... Pub names David Butterfield	66
Notes on... Signal boxes Christian Wolmar	68
Notes on... Motorways Mark Mason	69
Notes on... Brits in Paris Laura Freeman	70
Notes on... The Bank of England Mark Mason	72
Notes on... Ruins Harry Mount	73
Notes on... Ice cream Laura Freeman	74
Notes on... Soho drinking clubs Henry Jeffreys	75
Notes on... Marmalade Sophia Money-Coutts	76
Notes on... Tapestries Constance Watson	78
Notes on... Boxer shorts Justin Marozzi	79
Notes on... The Surrey Hills Christopher Winn	80
Notes on... The Cathars James Delingpole	81
Notes on... Wetherspoons Henry Jeffreys	82
Notes on... Doorsteps James Innes-Smith	84
Notes on... Ruislip Lido William Cook	85
Notes on... Pub quizzes Marcus Berkmann	86
Notes on... Corduroy Marcus Berkmann	88
Notes on... Hangovers Katy Balls	89
Notes on... A good night's sleep Laura Freeman	90
Notes on... Coming second Mark Mason	92
Notes on... Kites Christopher Fletcher	93
Notes on... Unst Ted Harrison	94

Notes on... Being the perfect guest Lucy Deedes	95
Notes on... Frankincense and myrrh David Abulafia	96
Notes on... Literary motorcycling Christopher Fletcher	98
Notes on... Wet weather boots Laura Freeman	99
Notes on... Book clubs Emily Rhodes	100
Notes on... Pigeon racing Jon Day	102
Notes on... Chinese porcelain Timothy Brook	103
Notes on... Hunting Camilla Swift	104
Notes on... Country house opera Guy Dammann	105
Notes on... Garden sculpture Prue Leith	106
Notes on... Visitors books Mary Killen	108
Notes on... Nominative determinism Dot Wordsworth	110
Notes on... Doner kebabs Michael Simmons	112
Notes on... The speaking clock Alan Steadman	114
Notes on... Ferret racing Peter Krijgsman	116
Notes on... St Nicholas Mary Wellesley	118
Notes on... Friday 13th Fergus Butler-Gallie	120
Notes on... Squatting Julie Bindel	122
Notes on... Lonely hearts ads Anthony Whitehead	124
Notes on... Metal detecting Nigel Richardson	126
Notes on... Fringes Martha Gill	128
Notes on... Whistling Steve Morris	130
Notes on... Tiramisu Tanya Gold	132
Notes on... Rude place names Hannah Tomes	134
Notes on... Treehouses Andrew Watts	136
Notes on... Aquariums Robert Porter	138
Notes on... Black tie Harry Mount	140
Notes on... Hedgehogs Tom Holland	141
Notes on... Quince Rod Liddle	142
Notes on... Historical re-enactments Christopher Brown	143
Notes on... Passport stamps Sean Thomas	144
Notes on... Lobsters Margaret Mitchell	146
Notes on... Going grey Cosmo Landesman	148
Notes on... Halloween turnips Melanie McDonagh	150
Notes on... Orcas Simon Barnes	152
Notes on... Bengal cats Miranda Morrison	154
Notes on... Italians Nicholas Farrell	156
Notes on... Cruise ship pianists Tom Yarwood	157
Notes on... Smoked salmon Henry Jeffreys	158
Notes on... Tarot reading Daisy Waugh	160
Notes on... Swiss Army knives Andrew Watts	162
Notes on... Rollies Ruari Clark	164
Notes on... Shrove Tuesday Francis Young	166
Notes on... Beef dripping Angus Colwell	168
Notes on... Ninjas Francis Pike	170
Notes on... Indexes Dennis Duncan	172
Index	174
Credits and Acknowledgements	176

Introduction

'Notes on…' was born of a slightly grubby accident. A little over a decade ago, *The Spectator*'s commercial department informed editorial that it would be easier to sell advertising to cruise liners and package holiday firms if we included a short dispatch from some pleasant part of the world. The idea was that readers would be so enamoured with the notion of a holiday that they would rush to book one of their own, preferably from companies that had chosen to advertise with us. So, for the first few years, that's what 'Notes on…' was: a half page towards the back of the magazine that ran pen portraits of, say, microbreweries in Kent or golfing holidays in the Algarve.

The promised advertising revenue never materialised and, while 'Notes on…' lost its function, the form remained: a short piece of no more than 600 words, wedged among the classified ads. Over the years, it became what it was always trying to be: a series of essays that find intrigue in the mundane.

And so we learn from the articles within this book – our 100 or so favourites from the past ten years – that most of the world's lab rats are the descendants of a single albino specimen born in 1906 in a scientific facility in Pennsylvania. Or that pebbles with a natural hole in their centre are known as 'adder stones' and were traditionally kept to ward off nightmares and witches. Or that the gold in the vault of the Bank of England cannot be stacked more than six bars high, otherwise it will sink into the clay on which Threadneedle Street was built. How wonderfully tangential that what started as a sop to advertisers became a home for such eclectic knowledge.

In some sense, 'Notes on…' is a revival of the very earliest iterations of *The Spectator*: the almanac or miscellany. It is not an overstatement (or, at least, not too much of one) to claim that it is this style of writing – disconnected meditations on everyday life – that started the Renaissance.

When paper first arrived in Europe, many Florentines started keeping what were known as *zibaldone*, personal miscellanies of everything from Bible verses and poetry to recipes and diary entries. Cheap paper meant artists could practise sketching, experimenting with composition and perspective, moving western art from the blocky flatness of Byzantine icons to the humanity of Giotto and later Botticelli. Mathematics and bookkeeping could be practised at length, without wasting expensive parchment or vellum, allowing the construction of ever more elaborate cathedrals and bridges. All of which existed within the *zibaldone*, alongside short descriptions of anything you could think of. Notes and books of notes changed the world.

But we digress. And that is precisely the joy of 'Notes on…'. It is the place within our pages where brief digression is the point. When *The Spectator* was revived in the early 19th century, it promised its readers not only 'miscellaneous information' but also that it would be 'a bundle of intelligence germinating hands and eyes in all directions – the hands springing out like the sons of earth, each armed with a pen'. The late Alexander Chancellor made the same point more concisely after he became editor in 1975. When he was asked what his 'policy' for the magazine was going to be, he replied: 'Well, we should publish some good articles, I suppose.' We hope that we have kept that spirit of rambling precision alive.

William Moore and Gus Carter

Notes on... Canapés
Ysenda Maxtone Graham

Canapés are one of life's delights and surprises – surprises because drinks party invitations usually give nothing away. Perhaps because 'nibbles' is such a hideous word, or perhaps just because of invitation convention, hosts tend simply to put 'Drinks, 6.30 to 8.30' on the Paperless Post card. So you arrive with no idea whether you're in for two hours of fizz on an empty stomach, or for a culinary treat in a succession of miniatures.

Always braced for the worst-case scenario – starvation in high heels – I'm overjoyed to spot a tray of canapés coming towards me through the throng, and am pathetically grateful to the host for this beneficence. For women, especially, eternally trying not to eat too much, canapés enable the perfect combination of two hours of active greed, while still not having as much to eat as you normally would for supper.

'Little bites of heaven' is how caterers portray canapés in their publicity material; and they're right. Written descriptions of the items, such as Emily Preece's sublime miniature 'Pork and nduja sausage rolls, bloody Mary ketchup' don't do justice to their mood-enhancing delectableness.

I've trained myself to hold back from grabbing a canapé too desperately when the tray comes round. I notice that the tactic of the unashamed is to be the first in the group of chatterers to grab and gobble one up, so that by the time the last person has had one (especially if they come with a dip, so it all takes longer), the first one has finished his (it usually is a he), and says: 'Ooh, may I have a second one?' I worry about this double-gobbling, because the conventional allocation is 12 canapés per person, at about £2 to £2.75 per canapé. So that person who has just stuffed £5 into his mouth in those 15 seconds has already had a sixth of his evening's allocation. For the whole thing to balance out, you need to count on a few thin women resolutely saying 'no thank you' for the entire evening.

What happens when the tray does arrive but there's only one canapé left on it? Who takes it? One thing is certain: everyone wants it. But there's usually a brief time of hesitation, during which a sort of dance takes place, the men politely saying 'you first' to the women, and the women knowing they couldn't live with themselves if they succumbed to such a public act of greed. Usually, in the end, it's the fattest of the men who pops it into his mouth with a gracious shrug.

The only thing that mars the canapés experience for me is the arrival of the sweet canapés, which have become fashionable. They're the equivalent of the neon lights being switched on towards the end of a teenage disco: 'Not much longer, folks!' The imminent end of the party is signalled. There's a strange hybrid time when the last of the savoury ones are still going round, and the first of the sweet ones have arrived, and you know that as soon as you've had your first sweet one, you can never, ever go back. To eat a miniature brownie at 8.15 p.m. is not only goodbye to the party, but also death to the evening ahead.

Notes on... Jeans   William Moore

North Korea has a problem with Alan Titchmarsh's crotch. In 2024, an old episode of *Garden Secrets* was aired on state television, but the network blurred Titchmarsh from the waist down. The offence was his gardening trousers – a pair of jeans. For the Workers' Party of Korea, jeans represent an 'invasion of capitalistic lifestyles'. They must be resisted.

In a sense, Kim Jong-un is right that jeans are a sign of American dominance. In 1986 the philosopher Régis Debray declared there was 'more power in blue jeans and rock 'n' roll than the entire Red Army'. Communist states agreed. Western-produced jeans were banned in the Soviet Union and Maoist China. The smuggling of bootleg jeans became so widespread that Soviet authorities gave it its own name – 'jeans crime'. A single pair could be sold for as much as a month's average salary. In the mid-1970s there were attempts in East Germany to manufacture state-approved alternatives to American jeans, but without much success. As one disgruntled reader wrote to *Pravda*: 'When you can make jeans better than Levi's, that will be the time to start talking about national pride.'

Yet when it comes to the idolisation of jeans, nothing can top country music. The association of jeans with blue-collar work and cowboy individualism is irresistible to many country stars, as spoofed by the comedian Bo Burnham in 'Country Song (Pandering)': 'A cold night/ A cold beer/ A cold jeans.' The strongest example of sincere jeans worship comes from Zac Brown in his 2003 song 'Chicken Fried'. He cites 'a pair of jeans that fit just right' as one of the things that American troops fight and die to protect.

Giorgio Armani said that jeans represent democracy in fashion because anyone can wear them, but is that true? Jeans have been part of the uniform for every western youth culture movement of modern times (skinheads and hippies; rappers and punks; goths and hipsters), but there's an unsettling feeling when you see someone in their off-duty jeans, like bumping into your teacher at the weekend.

In 2018, 'researchers' from CollectPlus made the unverifiable claim that 53 was the maximum age someone could get away with jeans. The truth is that while age, attractiveness and politics may all be factors, who can and can't wear them is an instinctual judgment. Ronald Regan could wear jeans; Richard Nixon couldn't.

Confession: I don't own a pair of jeans. I once told this to a Montanan cowboy. He looked at me as if I'd told him I don't own a toothbrush. Unlike Kim, my dislike isn't ideological, it's visceral. Jeans may be timeless, but their different iterations are not. I blame my prejudice on the style that was popular when I was teenager in the early 2000s. Then, the fashion for boys' jeans was big, baggy and deliberately ripped, worn so they hung around the

thighs. I was inoculated against them forever, like a bad oyster.

Still, while I don't own a pair, and I'll keep to corduroys and chinos, I'm grateful jeans exist, because they led to some nifty innovations. For instance, jeans were the first trouser to feature an 'Amazing Hookless Fastener' – or, as it was later renamed, a zip.

Notes on... Carps Jon Day

All anglers are obsessive, but carp fishers are the most single-minded of all. They think nothing of spending weeks on the banks of a muddy lake or gravel pit, lines and breath baited, waiting for a bite. Ask an aficionado what motivates him and he'll speak – with an intensity that sounds a lot like love – about the carp's unrivalled cunning and fighting ability: its coquettish, crafty takes and its long, blistering runs. Most of all he will talk in awe about the sheer, meaty heft of these fish, of their unparalleled weight and girth.

Carp fishing is a particularly British obsession, which is surprising, as the species is a relative newcomer to our waters. In *The Compleat Angler*, first published in 1653, Izaak Walton described the carp as 'the queen of rivers; a stately, a good, and a very subtil fish', and asserted that the species had been brought to England only 100 or so years previously by one 'Mr Mascal, a gentleman that then lived at Plumsted in Sussex, a county that abounds more with this fish than any in this nation'. (In fact it seems likely that carp arrived on these shores sometime in the 14th century.)

In Walton's day carp were primarily for eating – their tolerance for poor quality water meant they could be easily bred in large stock ponds, often attached to monasteries – but these days it's all catch and release. Carp are the prized target of coarse anglers, who treat them more as pets than as quarry. When a carp angler catches one he will lay it tenderly on a cushioned mat (pre-wetted so as not to damage the fish's coating of protective slime) before delicately unhooking it. He will apply antiseptic salve to its lips, then pose for photographs, cradling his catch with all the pride of a new father.

Many of the largest carp in Britain have become celebrities. They're given names; their vital statistics are recorded as assiduously as a supermodel's. For years the heaviest was 'Two Tone', a huge common who lived in Conningbrook Lake in Kent. Two Tone was a wily fish, caught once or twice a year, which only made him more alluring. When he was found floating – dead – on the surface of the lake in 2010, anglers from across the country came out to mourn.

Carp have only got bigger in the decade since, caused in part by better husbandry and care, but also by more intense feeding, which has created some consternation in the carp fishing world. Catching 40lb-plus fish used to be big news, but now there are around 1,000 fish over that weight in British waters. Whether these monstrous fish represent a sporting challenge is endlessly debated in the specialist press.

In 2021, a 14-year-old angler named Jensen Price landed a 73lb fish (the weight of a ten-year-old child) named 'Marshall' from a Cambridgeshire fishery. His claim on the record was denied by the British Record Fish Committee because, they argued, 'the weights stated for the overall population of carp in the fishery are unsustainable in a naturally fed venue, where the only additional food source is anglers' bait'. You wonder what Walton would have made of a catch like that.

Notes on... Land Rovers Ben Fogle

At the funeral for Prince Philip, Duke of Edinburgh, his coffin was carried in a Land Rover. Not any old Land Rover, but a Defender 130 Gun Bus, designed by the Duke for his funeral and adapted by Foley Specialist Vehicles. By chance, years ago, when researching my book on Land Rovers, I visited Foley while they were adapting the Duke's vehicle. I had to sign a non-disclosure agreement forbidding me from discussing the car until after his death.

First, a little history. The Land Rover was launched in 1948 as a farm vehicle to help re-establish Britain's shattered economy through agriculture. It cost £450 and was later named the Series I. This was followed by the Series II, IIA and III and then the 110, 90, 127 and the Defender, the name now used to refer to the entire 'boxy' lineage of cars.

Unlike other vehicles, no two Land Rovers are the same, even if they have rolled off the same factory line together. A Defender is like a Lego car. It might arrive in kit form, but it doesn't take long before it is adapted into a bespoke, personalised vehicle. Grilles are changed, seats reconfigured, lights added, step plates, ladders and roof racks installed. A whole market for post-production modification was born through the utility vehicle's adaptability.

Land Rovers carried marines into battle in the Falklands and ferried casualties from Iraq. They were used by the Israelis to dupe the Ugandans into releasing the hostages from the Entebbe hijacking, and by the thieves in the Great Train Robbery. They served on the front line in Northern Ireland (they are back on the streets now) and were once found on every farm in the country.

No other car has mastered the art of being classless. They are as at home on a farm as a country estate. They are beloved of rock 'n' roll royalty, gangsters, dictators and footballers. Bob Marley loved his. Winston Churchill and Che Guevara loved theirs.

The royal Land Rover lineage has a long pedigree. The Royal Yacht Britannia had a blue Land Rover Series 1 for overseas tours. For the late Duke of Edinburgh, the Land Rover Defender was his primary mode of transport during numerous overseas tours.

And therein lies the significance in his choice of hearse. The Land Rover was a part of Philip's private and public life for 70 years. And his posthumous request has precedent. It may surprise people to learn that dedicated Land Rover hearse companies have been established over the years for farmers, soldiers and explorers. Even the Co-op offers a burial service with one.

Despite the array of high-spec vehicles owned by the royal family, the Defender remains their favourite. It is said Queen Elizabeth II designed hers with windscreen wipers on the inside to wipe away the condensation made by her dogs.

Notes on... Big Ben Mark Mason

That silly debate at the start of 2020 over whether Big Ben should bong to mark Brexit wasn't the first time the famous bell had caused consternation. Listeners to a BBC radio news bulletin in 1949 were horrified when the chimes failed to sound. They had to wait until a later bulletin for an explanation: the clock was running four minutes slow because a swarm of starlings had gathered on the minute hand.

In fact, right from the start there were problems with the Great Bell. (That's its official name – 'Big Ben' is a nickname honouring, depending on who you believe, either Sir Benjamin Hall, who oversaw its installation, or Benjamin Caunt, a heavyweight boxer.) The original bell, cast in Stockton-on-Tees, cracked during tests in New Palace Yard. A replacement was made at the Whitechapel Bell Foundry, and carried to Westminster through cheering crowds on a trolley drawn by 16 horses. It began striking on 11 July 1859, but within two months it too had developed a crack. A lighter hammer was installed (even this one weighs a fifth of a ton), and the bell was turned slightly so the strike occurred in a different place. The crack is there to this day.

Big Ben's note is an E (though changes in official concert pitch since the 19th century make it closer to a modern F). Four smaller bells play the tune just before the hour is struck. One of these (the B note) is needed twice in quick succession, meaning the hammer doesn't have time to reset, so there's another hammer on the opposite side. The tune has words: 'All through this hour, Lord be my Guide. And by thy power, no foot shall slide.'

Do book yourself in for a tour of the Elizabeth Tower when they restart after the current renovation works are completed. You get to stand just a few feet from Big Ben as it rings out, so make sure you do the tour that finishes at midday – more bong for your buck, or rather for your no buck, as the tours are free. You can also see the microphone that carries the sound to the BBC for its live transmissions (though of course at the moment it is using a recording).

The fact that Auntie broadcasts the bongs live was of crucial importance in a 1967 episode of *Captain Scarlet*. In 'Big Ben Strikes Again', the puppet hero had to find a location where someone had reported hearing the clock strike 13. His colleague Captain Blue realised that this let them compute the distance from parliament – the delayed sound waves from the bell must have been striking exactly in sync with the bongs as heard on the radio. So the 13th bong was simply a 'real' repeat of the 12th one already heard over the airwaves.

The discrepancy arises because radio waves travel at the speed of light rather than the speed of sound (186,000 miles per second versus 760 miles per hour). So you should also perform the delightful experiment of standing at the bottom of the Elizabeth Tower (on the pavement opposite Westminster

Tube), listening to the bongs on Radio 4 (analogue rather than digital – the latter is slightly delayed). You hear Big Ben on the radio before you hear it for real. Sounds impossible, but I've tried it, and I promise you it's true.

Notes on... Mothing Mark Solomons

As darkness falls, a group of mainly middle-aged men set up traps of various shapes and sizes – some sophisticated and expensive-looking, others more Heath Robinson-like – in gardens and fields across the country. These are moth enthusiasts: a largely unknown and, by their very nature, unseen group of hobbyists. They are mostly fanatical birdwatchers too, and from backgrounds that include journalism, the civil service, the Royal Mail and the NHS.

They lay their traps, some of which cost £500 or more, throughout most of the year. In the mornings they count, identify and list their catch in minute detail. The moths are then carefully released, away from prowling blackbirds who turn up when they think there's a chance of an easy meal.

Most traps use actinic bulbs, which emit bright UV light to attract the moths. The moths then flutter into a plastic or wooden container beneath and crawl, dazed but unharmed, into empty egg boxes until the morning.

My local group is the Eel's Footmen, a play on words combining the name of the local pub – The Eel's Foot – with the footman family of moths that includes dusky, scarce, dingy and four-dotted. And if you think those are names to conjure with, just wait till you get to the wainscots, old lady, dark arches and, my favourite, the setaceous Hebrew character – if ever I write an autobiography, that's my title right there.

There is an overwhelming desire among moth lovers to compile as long a list as possible, including names in both English and Latin, as well as dates, times, locations, habitat and weather conditions. When the moth-catchers came to my garden and enquired about habitat, I said it was a former country cottage with some modernisation. They didn't laugh. Mothing is a serious business. What I apparently should have said, though, was 'acid grassland with nearby reedbeds'.

As with twitchers, some moth-catchers travel vast distances to clap eyes on a rare specimen or anything officially 'notifiable' – meaning that it goes into the county record as a rare example or first for the area.

Lists are vital in keeping a record of whether numbers are going up or down. This is important in an area such as ours on the Suffolk coast where habitats are threatened by the proposed new Sizewell C nuclear power station. It is also eye-opening for those of us who previously thought of moths only as pests that ate clothes or fluttered round our light bulbs when the windows were left open.

The colours and markings are remarkable, from the delicate patterns on the tiniest micro moths which make up most of the 2,500 species in the UK, to the bright green of the emerald moth – a beauty wasted on most of us by coming out in the dark.

The Eel's Footmen have put their traps in my garden three times in the past six months and netted 138 different species: among them, the red underwing, lobster, spectacle, elephant hawk-moth and the twig-like buff tip – not to mention the less romantically named turnip moth. The best find was, I'm told, a *Dichomeris alacella*. It wasn't much to look at compared with some of the others, but it was notifiable.

Notes on... Croquet Sam Leith

People say cricket is the quintessential English game. Those people are wrong. Cricket may have a longer pedigree, but it's too boring, too democratic and too honourable to qualify: croquet is the game that truly captures what it is to be English. As any pub quizzer will tell you, Wimbledon started its life in 1868 as the All England Croquet Club, only developing its vulgar sideline in lawn tennis late in the following decade. Its reputation has yet to recover.

Just like cricket, where the game as played on the village green differs from the international game, the echt English croquet is the one played, ideally slightly drunk, in the echt Englishman's garden. Its idiosyncrasies are what makes it special. For me, the only true croquet lawn in the world will always be the threadbare triangle of grass in the middle of Weston's Yard in Eton.

A perfect croquet lawn – should such a thing exist – would make the game a cousin of billiards; a thing of unforgivingly precise geometry, governed by the Newtonian rules of particle mechanics. Touch, feel and low cunning would be all but irrelevant. The special joy of the game as played at home is that the lawn is imperfect. This confers a home advantage (you learn how to correct for the slight dent on the approach to the second hoop; you know where clover makes the grass slow; you know which slightly bent hoop won't tolerate anything but a perpendicular approach) and leads to a proliferation of house rules; which, set correctly, will also confer a home advantage.

Two no-nos. The golf-shot (mallet perpendicular to feet) makes you look a wally and doesn't do your accuracy any favours. And putting your foot on your own ball when you play a croquet shot is just awful, and probably against the rules.

Played properly, croquet is the greatest game of co-operation and sabotage to be found on earth. There really is no point at all playing it – as some do – with each player taking a mallet and ball and going it on their own. When you play in teams, the game opens up – it transforms the mallet-and-ball equivalent of snap into a game of contract bridge.

The trick is to leave opponents so far away from you and from each other that any flailing long-distance attempt to roquet your ball is, effectively, a donation of their ball to you for further punishment. The satisfaction of sending your despairing opponent's ball trundling right up to, but not into, a distant flowerbed… that may be the second greatest pleasure on earth. The greatest being that of quietly, helpfully, patronisingly, putting your teammate through hoop after hoop without his getting a mallet to his own ball. This really is a 'zero-sum game': the less your opponents and even teammates are enjoying it, the more you will be. Your glory is another's fury.

Croquet was Auberon Waugh's game, which says it all. Friends who visited Combe Florey, his Somerset home, report that he was a fiercely competitive player. That is, he cheated like mad – even after having disadvantaged his guests with strong Bloody Marys before play began. That is quite proper. The day the Englishman can no longer cheat at croquet in his own back garden is the day this ceases to be a land fit for heroes.

Notes on... Invitations Philip Womack

The other day, clearing out boxes, I stumbled on a sheaf of invitations from childhood. Decorated with trains and fairies, they are very similar to those my children still (just about) receive today, except there's usually a Thelwell pony instead of Elsa from *Frozen*. The handwritten addresses, the names of the houses and streets (Bluebell Cottage, Leeward Road) plunged me back to 1980s Sussex, sunlit gardens and pass the parcel (where only the winner got a prize, unlike now, when a Haribo lurks in every layer).

It was a ritual. There was the pleasure of choosing the invitations ('Darling, we had spaceships last year'), the thrill of doling them out and the tension of waiting for the RSVPs. It was also, though I knew it not at the time, social preparation. In my final year at prep school, the headmaster issued us with a formal invitation to drinks. We had

to respond properly, or we could not attend. Cue little boys scribbling variations on 'I delightedly accept your wondrous invitation'. We were demurred. The answer, of course, was to use the third person. 'Philip Womack thanks…' We were allowed to go to the party anyway. We also learned our lesson. A creamy, thick, engraved and gilded card: who would go to the trouble now? On my mantelpiece sit a brace: to dinner at a livery company, and to a wedding. They are lonely. I wonder if I will have to leave them there, after the dates have passed. A faux pas, I know, but what can you do? An invitation to a garden party at Buckingham Palace stood in situ for several years, until eventually even I had to agree it was time to put it away. Perhaps we can extend the rule to a month afterwards, given their scarcity.

Some may balk at using the word 'invite', though Bishop Cranmer would disagree. I admit to printing out an evite (etymologically, the 'e' points to the opposite of 'invite': an 'outvite') from the Archbishop of Canterbury, so I could rest it casually against the photographs. What else are mantelpieces for? You can chart lives by invitations. At university they requested us to twenty-firsts, to drinks parties, to balls, with that wonderful injunction: carriages at midnight. One dining club sent cards in the shape of a skull. It's hard now to remember why we all yearned for one, a *memento mori* if ever there was; but yearn we did.

The physical invitations fluttered in throughout my twenties: book launches, At Homes, engagements, weddings, each offering anticipation (who'll be there?) and anxiety (will I embarrass myself?), delights and, more often than not, hungover drives down the M4, not, usually, in a carriage.

Your standard invitation now creeps in, harum-scarum among your emails, between an offer for discounted earplugs on Amazon and a Substack you've forgotten you'd subscribed to. What's more, they have a habit of diminishing into the ether. You try searching for one on your way to a party. The saddest thing about this electronic trend is that communal activities become surreptitious. Children's parties are organised by WhatsApp, which excludes the child. And so, to hosts everywhere (and no sniggering please): Philip Womack requests – no, demands – the pleasure. Bring back the stiffy!

Notes on... Obituaries Mark Mason

My obituaries habit gets ever stronger. I find there's nothing as inspiring or instructive or entertaining as reading a few hundred words about someone's time on this planet. My main dealers are the *Times* and Radio 4's *Last Word*. Each batch throws together a varied mix, people who share only one thing in common: the fact that they checked out at the same time. All human life is here, as it were.

A good obituary knows we want stories, not lists of achievements. Some obituaries read like sitcom scripts. Like the obit for a rugby hero who played in a match between the British army of the Rhine and the French army. Twelve players were sent off, one of them our hero for landing a right hook on the nose of an opponent who had just bitten him on the genitals. Or the father of Michael Bond (he of *Paddington*), who on family holidays in the Isle of Wight would insist on wearing his hat in the sea in case he needed to raise it to anyone.

Others read like thrillers. A policeman involved in the Yorkshire Ripper inquiry despaired of his boss's contempt for suggestions – such as that of a colleague who thought the killer drove a lorry because footprints showed one of his heels was more worn than the other. Peter Sutcliffe was indeed a lorry driver. Sometimes you're left wondering. A billionaire set up a trust fund from which his children then gradually excluded him, leaving him and his wife to pen a book that ended with the line 'Our nightmare will never end'. But the obit didn't really get to the bottom of why they fell out. Perhaps no one could, not even the family themselves. Families are like that.

Occasionally I'll feel sad when someone's obit was the first I'd ever heard of them and I like the sound of them. As soon as they're here they're gone, as though you've been allowed to shake their hand once and once only. But there will still be their work to check out, their films or music or whatever. And in one way the fact they've experienced the Great Leveller makes you feel closer to them. It always reminds me of the gravestone in the crypt of St-Martin-in-the-Fields: 'Remember man as thou goest by, As thou art now so once was I, As I am now so must thou be, Prepare thy self to follow me.'

Sometimes batches of obits can produce lovely coincidences. Last year, next to each other on the same page in the *Times*, were Karl Wallinger, whose royalties from Robbie Williams's cover of his song 'She's The One' got him through a serious illness, and Peter McCann, who founded the rehab clinic at which Williams himself saw a mural of some angels and was inspired to write his best-known song.

The ages within a batch remind you that 'three score years and ten' is just an estimate, one that comes without a guarantee. A recent page covered people who'd died at 89,

83 and 55. But sometimes there are pleasing patterns – Nicholas Parsons and Murray Walker dying at 96 and 97 respectively, having been born on the same day as each other in 1923. And the obit of Ken Capstick, Arthur Scargill's right-hand man, finished with the story of him texting Scargill on the day Margaret Thatcher died. The message read simply: 'Thatcher dead.' The reply was instant: 'Scargill alive.'

Notes on... Corkscrews Henry Jeffreys

For the first 50 years of the corked bottle, there was no easy way to get into it. The combination of cork and a strong glass bottle came together around 1630 but the first mention of a device to open the bloody thing wasn't until 1681. Cavalier get-togethers must have resembled the teenage parties I attended with everyone desperately trying to open the bottle using keys, pens, knives, etc. Or using that technique where you bang the bottle against a wall with the heel of a shoe. Halcyon days. More likely they'd just take the top off cleanly with a swift blow from a sabre and a loud 'Huzzah!'.

Early devices for extracting corks were called 'bottle screws'. According to Hugh Johnson, the word 'corkscrew' was first used in 1720. From there, this handy little piece of

equipment has conquered the world, from early versions which were simply a piece of metal with a wooden handle to the full nerdery of the £100 Screwpull – beloved by wine bores of a certain vintage. The most common one when I was taking my first steps as a wine drinker was the metal man with his hands up which usually just drilled a hole in the cork rather than removing it. As someone who has opened thousands of bottles of wine, I can safely say that the best corkscrew is a good quality waiter's friend pocketknife. I never leave home without one.

If you want to see the sheer imagination and thought that mankind has taken to remove a bit of tree bark from a glass receptacle, I'd highly recommend visiting the corkscrew museum (yes, there really is one, I literally have the T-shirt) at Domaine Gerovassiliou near Thessaloniki. There are corkscrews with winged demons on, others that look like medieval torture devices, and ones that fit into the top of walking canes, so a gentleman need never be without.

But at some point, will this essential piece of drinker's kit be seen only in a museum? According to a report from kitchenware retailer Lakeland, just over a quarter of 18- to 24-year-olds own a corkscrew – compared with 81 per cent of over-65s. I'm not entirely sure this is the killer statistic everyone thinks it is, though. One in three youngsters having a corkscrew means you're in with a very good chance of finding one in shared accommodation. We didn't all have our own corkscrew when I was in my early twenties. Well, I did. But I was a budding wine bore.

There's no doubt, however, that the traditional cork is dying out, thanks to the ubiquitous screw cap. This has gone from being seen only on the cheapest wines to an entirely respectable way to close a bottle, especially in the Antipodes. Something like 70 per cent of Australian and 95 per cent of New Zealand wines are sealed this way. Screw caps are more reliable too. It's estimated that between 3 and 8 per cent of corks are tainted with a compound called TCA (2,4,6-trichloroanisole) which produces the characteristic 'corked' smell of damp basements. Extremely annoying when you've been keeping a bottle for a special occasion.

And yet for all its occasional unreliability, I'll miss the cork when it finally disappears. A large part of the appeal of wine is the ritual of opening the bottle, the satisfying pop followed by the gurgle of the pour. It all builds anticipation. Now, where did I put my corkscrew?

Notes on... Routemasters   Paul Burke

At the former Chiswick Works in west London, I recently celebrated the Routemaster's 70th birthday. I owe my existence to this majestic mode of transport. My mum was a conductress on a Routemaster – the No. 16 – which cut a merry swathe from Cricklewood to Victoria, right through the centre of London. My dad, like a lot of young Irishmen, had arrived in London in the 1950s to help rebuild a city still recovering from the second world war. Every morning, he'd catch the first bus from his digs off the Edgware Road to various building sites. One morning he got chatting to the young clippie, and married her a few months later. 'Open the front door,' he'd say to me years later, 'and the whole world's outside.'

For families like ours, who didn't own a car, the 'whole world' began at the bus stop. Routemasters arrived at the end of our street to take us where we wanted to go. Passengers still pine for their perfect confluence of form and function. Each one was more than a

mere bus, it was a mobile community. Its open back platform allowed the locals to jump on and off swiftly.

My mum wasn't the only family member who worked on the No. 16. She and Uncle Ken, conductor and driver respectively, were London Transport's only brother-and-sister bus crew. Except when Uncle Ken was paired with his sister Gert or his sister Joyce. So for my family, *On the Buses* was less a sitcom and more a documentary.

On a Routemaster, the conductor ran the show. The best ones were like good publicans, greeting their regulars with a quip and a smile. They all had their rules and my mum's included 'Never take a fare from a nurse or a nun'. She also acted as a vital conduit between passengers who'd just arrived from Ireland or the Caribbean and needed somewhere to live, and other passengers who might have a spare room.

After dark, the sight of an approaching Routemaster was like a warm, welcoming lantern that had come to carry you home. Although you were never sure exactly when it was going to arrive, I believed – still do – that if you stared hard enough up the road, your bus would miraculously appear.

From an early age, I was hopping on without adult supervision. Kids round our way were all brought up with that ideal combination of love and neglect, so our mums neither knew nor cared where we went during school holidays. The first place was usually Franklin's newsagent, where we could buy a 25p ticket called a Red Rover and enjoy a day's unlimited bus travel on Routemasters.

Bus travel lost its magic when Routemasters, along with conductors, were phased out. They were replaced by lumbering one-man buses. Passengers were delayed because the driver had to take all the fares, then again because, without the open platform, they were trapped until the doors were released.

Socially and environmentally, London has suffered ever since. At Chiswick Works, I felt extraordinarily lucky. Without the Routemaster, I wouldn't be here. And without it, as a child, I wouldn't have been anywhere.

Notes on... Gins in tins Flora Watkins

I'm writing this in my car, laptop on knees and a delicious can of Tanqueray Flor de Sevilla gin and tonic in the drinks holder, while my sons are at cricket practice. It's an inclement evening, but were it a sunny summer's day, the Yummy Mummies would be sprawled around the boundary in their Veja trainers and prairie dresses, pastel-coloured tins in hand, cackling and catching up like some Gen X version of Hogarth's 'Gin Lane'.

Gins in tins are the acceptable form of 'mother's ruin'. First came Gordon's G&T in a tin, followed by its pink gin, and now the chiller aisle contains more temptation than the Haribo shelves do for my children.

Bombay Sapphire, Tanqueray, Sipsmith and multiple artisan brands have got in on the act. They're usually on offer at your preferred supermarket, with three for the price of four. That is, unless you plump for

supermarket-brand gin tins, which come in at about 99p each.

Gins in tins are part of the fastest-growing drinks markets, that of 'RTDs' (ready-to-drink cocktails). Post-pandemic, volume sales have outperformed white spirits, with the market estimated to have reached £884 million last year, according to Alice Baker, a senior research analyst at Mintel. And usage of RTDs is highest among the under-45s, she confirms. Perma-stressed working mothers like me now think little of cracking open a Sipsmith's canned G&T or Grey Goose vodka spritzer instead of putting the kettle on when they get in from the school run. One friend says: 'Gins in tins at 4 p.m. on a Friday was basically why I signed my son up for cricket. It's rude not to there.'

My grandparents' generation had the gin tray, brought out at 6 p.m.: cut-glass tumblers, vicious measures of Gordon's, half a bottle of flat Schweppes tonic water and some little dishes of salted crisps and Opies cocktail onions. Some older people, like my great friend Roger, an antiques dealer, continue this tradition – but after one of his tinctures I need to lie down. And that isn't the point of gins in tins: I don't want to get wasted (I've got some half-arsed parenting to do and possibly need to drive). What gins in tins provide is more akin to a socially acceptable form of Xanax or the Valium doled out to 1950s housewives: they just take the edge off endlessly bickering siblings and battles over homework.

The late Shirley Conran said that life was too short to stuff a mushroom. In the post-Brexit, post-pandemic era when the fantastic au pairs we once employed are a distant dream, frankly who has time to locate ice, the gin bottle and a can of Fever-Tree, only to find you've run out of lemons? A tin of chilled Bombay Collins (my current favourite: it tastes just like a piquant lemon barley water) consumed at a family flashpoint is one of the best life hacks I know.

RTDs are targeted at women. Portobello Road gin and tonic 'looks seriously swanky – you'll be the envy of the train with this in your hand!', reads a recent blind testing on the BBC Good Food website. One of the few male aficionados I know is my godfather, though he is fond of declaiming, 'a can of Gordon's gin and tonic is the perfect mixer for… a large measure of Gordon's'.

Notes on... Falconry Mark Cocker

In 2024, the Hollywood team making the latest *Mission Impossible* film was desperate to clear Trafalgar Square of its superabundant pigeons for a scene involving Tom Cruise. But it was not an ultrasonic laser in Ethan Hunt's high-tech kitbag that did the trick. What you apparently need to rid central London of its pesky birds is an artform dating back 3,000 years.

The producers had to resort to falconers to get the job done. These devotees of an ancient art, who have also performed sterling service recently for administrators at St Paul's Cathedral and the Palace of Westminster, let loose a 'cast' of red-tailed hawks, complete with bells and jesses, and sent the pigeons packing.

The tabloids made a splash on these old-style methods, but actually it is one of falconry's more modest contributions to the cultural life of the capital. Hunting with birds of prey arrived in Britain from Asia in about AD 900. Yet it took off with the Norman Conquest when every self-respecting wealthy Londoner had a 'cadge' (a technical hawking term for an enclosure) of falcons behind his residence in a building known as a 'mews'.

These structures may have been repurposed as horse stables once falconry fell from fashion in the Georgian period. Yet everyone who lives in one of the many terraces of mews today dwells where London's falcons would once have slept. Richard II's own version was in Charing Cross, but the famous royal mews belonging to the fanatical falconer Charles II stood on a site now occupied by the National Gallery.

In keeping with strict feudal hierarchy, the various raptors used in falconry were allocated according to social station. Generally, the bigger the bird, the higher the status. Eagles were reserved for those of imperial rank, but a fierce giant of the Arctic tundra known as a gyrfalcon was a predator of choice for kings.

Highborn women had to make do with the tiny falcon known as the merlin, albeit a suitably bejewelled creature with its own brand of bijou elan. Catherine the Great and Mary Queen of Scots were both said to be much taken with their merlins. To the lowest in society, however, went the lowly mouse-catching kestrel. A dying echo of that feudal allocation is commemorated in the title to Barry Hines's classic novel of thwarted working-class spirit, *A Kestrel for a Knave*.

For all the complex ritual that accreted around falconry, at its heart was a very practical business about delivering protein to the human diet. It was developments in firearm technology that eventually led guns to replace falcons as the hunter's weapon of choice. Yet birds of prey supplied a genuine need for more than a millennium. Hawks were sometimes trained to work in pairs so that they could tackle far bigger prey items. Herons and cranes, which formed an exalted centrepiece on the medieval banquet table, were routinely captured with these methods.

Perhaps the most remarkable and deepest factor at play in a practice that held Europe in thrall for so long – and is still a multi-billion dollar enterprise among the royal families of the Middle East – is something much more elemental.

It is a capacity to enter into a profound connection with a wild creature. Devotees often liken it to a marriage or a relationship between owner and slave, in which they are the servant. The bird itself is always master.

Notes on... Trainers Justin Marozzi

What is it with men and trainers? Or rather, men of a certain age and trainers. I'm still trying to banish the horror-show image of Rishi Sunak wearing Adidas Sambas in No. 10 in an interview to promote his tax policies.

Has western civilisation really come to this? Are we destined to succumb to rubber-soled hell, or is there still a place left for those of us who prefer shoes that last decades, not a couple of years before being consigned to the dustbin of athleisure history?

For years I've played a game checking out men's footwear on the London Underground. The proportion of trainers has risen exponentially, like grey squirrels stealing *lebensraum* from their indigenous red cousins, so that today you're lucky if you even spot a leather-soled shoe. I've even noticed three septuagenarian friends – a peer of the realm, a tycoon and a retired general – sneaking in black sneakers beneath a Savile Row suit.

I'm conflicted, of course. Part of me says, to hell with what everyone else is wearing. Stick to your sumptuous, handmade, Goodyear-welted beauties. And then the other part looks at a pair of On Cloudvistas or Hoka Bondi 8s and lusts after that all-day comfort – cloudlike cushioned cosiness, for heaven's sake – and whispers, give it to me, baby.

My shoe collection looks like a graveyard. I stare across the rows of wonderfully patinated, butter-soft leather boots, brogues and loafers by Henry Maxwell, Church's, Crockett & Jones, Cheaney, Tricker's and Alfred Sargent. An R.M. Williams or two for rugged, in-the-field manliness, here and there a more delicate Carmina or the surprisingly inexpensive Mocasines Pepe of Marbella

(good enough for the king of Spain, good enough for me) for a whiff of Spanish *estilo*. Is that a pair of black tassel loafers over there, relegated to the 'don't wear, will never wear, what was I ever thinking, but can't quite throw them out yet' category?

But wait, what's that? A pair of New Balance dad trainers, laddish Nike Air Force 1s and a feeble, misjudged attempt at the 'smart black trainer', the clumpy Camper Runner K21. I know. My wife was right.

I first dipped my toes, so to speak, in trainers years ago. That was because we had to. In the 1970s, trainers meant PE and PE meant running the gauntlet past a regularly rotating cast of prep school paedophiles. We all wore Dunlop Green Flashes, as first sported by Fred Perry half a century earlier. Looking back on it, they were crap. Later came Converse, another concession to American democratic wear, and although they always looked good, and still do, they were also crap. Wear them for a day and see how you feel. Later still came the obscenely comfortable Camper Pelotas in brown leather, but I'm not sure they were ever really trainers. I live in mine.

What's a man to do? In my mid-fifties confusion over how to navigate this sartorial wasteland, I consult my guru Stephen Bayley (who confesses to having forecast the demise of the trainer back in 1992). 'A hybrid sports-formal shoe, viz Prada, is now such a commonplace that establishments attempting to ban trainers in their dress code look like T-Rex seconds before the asteroid hit,' he says. 'But the only certain thing about taste is that it changes. So when our politicians pose in Adidas Sambas, I am predicting the return of brogues and spats.'

Notes on... Kippers Andrew Watts

I miss kippers. My wife won't let me eat them at home, and they have become a rarity in restaurants. I once stayed in a luxury hotel, and the manager was telling me that if I wanted anything – valet parking, room service, breakfast after 10.30 a.m. – I had only to ask. When I enquired if kippers were on the menu, he went as white as unsmoked cod and mumbled that the head of housekeeping had forbidden them because of the luxury soft furnishings.

But I have medical science on my side: a recent report in the *British Medical Journal* said that fish such as herring could save lives, and the planet. Nearly three-quarters of forage fish – those half-way up the food chain, between plankton and larger fish, like tuna or cod – that are caught are not eaten,

but made into fish meal for farmed fish like salmon. Cutting out the middle-fish and eating forage fish themselves would be more efficient, sustainable and – because they contain omega-3 fatty acids – could save 750,000 lives if they replaced red meat in our diet. Also – and it's a shame the scientists didn't make more of this – herring tastes better than farmed salmon, the most boring fish on the market.

One of the problems is that these fish do not last: those who bought fresh herring from cadgers before refrigerators found that it was inedible as often as not, which is why 'cadger' now means 'someone who gets something for nothing' rather than its original meaning of 'a hawker of fish'. The only way to keep herring edible, if not palatable, was by heavily salting the fish and smoking it for nearly two months. The herring took on a red colour and a smell so overpowering that foxhounds could be put off the scent – hence the term 'red herring'.

The kipper was an invention of the railway age. When inland cities could be reached in hours, herring only needed to be lightly salted and smoked. The more romantic story is that in 1843 John Woodger in Northumberland split and gutted a herring ready for breakfast and left it overnight near a smoking stove; the result was so delicious that he had to share it. His smokehouse – conveniently enough, he had one handily situated for both the fishing village of Seahouses in Northumberland and the North-Eastern Railway – is still in operation.

Now, as then, the herring are 'cold smoked' – placed at a distance from a slow-burning fire, fuelled by sawdust and woodchips. Oak is best, but some smokers cut it with other wood; as long as there is some oak among the deadwood it can be described as 'oak-smoked'. This seems less of a cheat than the first world war trick of painting kippers with a dye made from coal tar to cut the time spent in the smokehouse.

This wartime expediency was the beginning of the end of the kipper. From its place on every Victorian and Edwardian breakfast table, it became the food of the poor – George Orwell writes in *The Road to Wigan Pier* about a supper of kippers and strong tea – and the Ministry of Agriculture was worried about what to do with all the herring. Civil servants wanted to distribute it free to schoolchildren – this is what they'd done with the oversupply of milk until Mrs Thatcher snatched it away – but the minister refused, saying: 'You cannot feed necessitous children on raw salt herring. I can imagine nothing which would upset a child more.'

The Herring Industry Board lasted until 1981, when Mrs Thatcher got rid of it too. I hope the *BMJ*'s scientists have more success.

Notes on... Wassailing Matthew Dennison

Before the Industrial Revolution shrank Christmas celebrations to two days, many workers across rural England might have spared a minute or two over Christmastide to bring out the family wassail bowl. Wassailing – sometimes in houses, sometimes in apple orchards – was a ceremonial toast to the health of friends, family and neighbours, or a ritualised routing of the bad spirits that lurk among fruit trees. Orchard wassailing, intended to guarantee bumper crops in the year ahead, was a rambunctious affair of gunshots, the banging together of trays and buckets and the blowing of cow horns (to scare away evil spirits), singing, drinking and bonfires. Amid the bucket-banging, harvesters found time to bow deeply in front of their chosen trees, which they afterwards toasted in cider, taking care to pour a little on to the tree roots.

In other instances, wassailing seems to have formed an element of a festive house party. Family and guests toasted one another in rank order, beginning with the master of the house. At-home wassailing, which was widespread across England and Scotland, required only bonhomie and warm spicy booze in a bowl.

Earliest instances of wassailing probably passed unrecorded. The tradition may even predate Christianity in these islands. The name comes from the Anglo-Saxon 'wes hal' or 'waes hael', meaning 'be whole' and so 'of good health': from the outset the drinking of a toast probably played a central part. The tradition seems to have been chiefly associated with Twelfth Night. On 17 January (the old Twelfth Night, before the introduction of the Gregorian Calendar), medieval revellers, led by a nominated 'King of the Wassailers', toured manors, taking with them the steaming wassail bowl and a buoyant sense of seasonal expectation, much in the manner of modern carollers. There was a song, the Wassail Song, with many regional variants.

Like all the best English traditions, wassailing kept a sharp eye on social niceties. Villagers who drank to their local worthy or feudal master were rewarded with gifts of food and money. Roasted apples were proffered to be dipped into the wassail bowl.

What did wassailers drink? It was cider for the orchard workers, while door-to-door wassailers traditionally drank a heady concoction called lambswool, which was made from hot, sweet, spiced ale thickened with a mixture of beaten cream, eggs and fluffy roasted apples, the resulting white frothiness inspiring its name. This is the

drink stipulated by the 17th-century poet Robert Herrick in 'Twelfth Night: or, King and Queen'. Here he identifies sugar, nutmeg and ginger as key ingredients.

Has the time come for a wassailing revival? What jollier symbol could there be of post-pandemic festivities than a bowl of hot sweetened grog paraded from house to house, with any number of revellers drinking their fill from the single vessel? Perhaps Jesus College, Oxford, will lead the way. The college's 18th-century silver-gilt wassail bowl, known as the Swig, can hold ten gallons of lambswool.

Notes on... Foie gras Paul Levy

A poll shows that nine out of ten Brits want to ban the import of foie gras. Crumbs! Haven't they got anything more important to worry about? The *Times* says about 200 tons are imported from Europe every year. I only wish some would come my way. Though the same article says Waitrose stocks this greatest of all delicacies, I can't remember seeing it in our local branch.

The trouble is that the campaign against these large, buttery duck livers (goose liver is rare) is based on Yahoo-worthy ignorance and antique disinformation, such as the fading photographs that used to circulate of webbed feet nailed to the shed floor. While I haven't been able to discover the extent of industrial foie gras production, what one

encounters in France is mostly artisanal, produced on farms, not factories.

As for 'force-feeding', it all depends on what you think this means. Certainly, the birds are encouraged to over-eat; gorging themselves in the autumn when there is a glut of food is the way these waterfowl prepare themselves for migration in nature. But I have witnessed the gavage, as the feeding process is called. I'm sorry to distress the anti-foie gras fanatics, but the birds are conditioned to queue up in an orderly fashion to swallow the feeding tube. They are not distressed, because ducks and geese do not have a gag reflex. The moistened grains that are the birds' breakfast, lunch and dinner are pushed through a sort of food mill into the metal tube, direct to the stomach. If they could speak, they might complain of the monotony of their diet.

They are kept in relatively capacious pens, as individual small pens are being phased out in the EU. And far from being handled sadistically by peasant women, the birds are petted as they receive their rations from the farmers' wives. Using force to feed them would obviously be counter-productive, as the object is to pack in the food without damage to the birds' beaks or organs.

Is there cruelty involved? Not in the gavage itself, though no animal could be said to enjoy having an enlarged, fatty liver. How much this subtracts from the quality of the birds' relatively short life is a question I leave to philosophers/zoologists. Are we justified in using these over-fed ducks as food for ourselves? Well, mankind has done so since antiquity. Foie gras was a luxurious delicacy for the Egyptians, the Romans and the former Hebrew slaves. Moreover, the rest of the bird is not squandered: it's not just the liver that is eaten. Particularly in south-western France, the breasts of foie gras ducks are a cherished menu item, and the legs lend themselves to making delicious confit de canard.

Ideological vegetarians and vegans have a case for not eating foie gras, but then they have a case for not eating anything that has a face or a mother. Meat is murder and all that.

But I wish the people who spend so much effort trying to ban foie gras would transfer their hysteria to some less trivial causes. Genuine foie gras is very expensive. Could it be that opposition to producing, selling and consuming it has some element of class war about it?

Notes on... Ordnance Survey maps
Mark Mason

You could say it started because of the French. The turmoil caused by their revolution got the British military worried about the possibility of an invasion, so maps of the 'invasion coast' (beginning with Kent in 1801) were produced. Hence the name 'Ordnance Survey'. Until the 1960s every director general of the agency held an army rank.

The first five-mile baseline from which everything was measured had been laid out earlier by Major-General William Roy, its two ends marked by cannons stuck in the ground. Coincidentally one of these lay just outside what is now Heathrow. It's still there. Searching for it once, I asked a planespotter if he knew where it was. He gave me a look that said: 'You nerd.' Which I found a tad rich.

There has always been a magic about OS maps. In *Dracula* (1897), Jonathan Harker notes that 'I was not able to light on any map or work giving the exact locality of the Castle Dracula, as there are no maps of this country as yet to compare with our own Ordnance Survey maps'.

In previous centuries technology meant a theodolite perched on a 'trig point', one of the concrete triangulation pillars installed across the country. These days it's satellites and aircraft, and artificial intelligence. The OS recently worked with Microsoft on technology that can identify different types of roof from aerial photos. The agency also supplies millimetre-accurate data for driverless tractors so they can work the fields day and night.

This sort of precision requires vigilance. The OS makes 20,000 changes a day to its database – a new house there, a change in the route of a fence there. The emergency services might need to know about the latter when they're trying to reach someone.

But as well as all its serious work the agency also revels in good old-fashioned silliness. It has worked out the longest straight line you can walk in Britain without crossing a road (44 miles, in the Cairngorms). It has ascertained where Britain would balance if you put it on a pin: Brennand Farm, four miles northwest of Dunsop Bridge in Lancashire. And it has created a map of Britain in Minecraft. This took 22 billion blocks.

Indeed, the OS is now like James Bond: the world is not enough. The agency was employed by Nasa to produce a map of Mars, and has also done the moon. Following in a tradition of OS cartographers writing themselves into maps (look closely and you'll see some of the cliffs at Blackgang on the Isle of Wight spell 'Bill'), the agency's Paul Naylor hid his own name in the lunar surface. He won't tell anyone where.

Digital maps are wonderful, and of course the OS should be leading the way. But there will always be something thrilling about heading out on a walk with one of their Explorer maps.

And everything comes full circle in the end. The OS started with the French – and William Roy's house on London's Argyll Street became a French Connection shop.

Notes on... The coronation spoon
Robert Tombs

A spoon may seem too homely for grand ceremony. It might even, in this sceptical and utilitarian age, seem slightly ridiculous. This prompts the question of how, or whether, we value ancient traditions and ceremonies whose original meanings and power are largely lost to us. And if we do value them, why?

This particular spoon, undeniably, is a very special one: doubtless the world's most important spoon, and certainly one of the most beautiful examples of that humble genus: silver-gilt, finely engraved with acanthus scrolls, decorated with pearls, and with its bowl strangely divided into two. It dates from the 12th century, and may have been used ever since Richard the Lionheart. It is the oldest piece of the coronation regalia.

After the Civil War the new republic melted everything down. The spoon alone was saved by a Mr Kinnersley, who bought it for 16 shillings – £3,000 today – and presented it to the restored Charles II. It holds the oil that anoints each sovereign (hence the divided bowl, for the archbishop's two fingers), re-enacting the Biblical anointing of King Solomon by Zadok the Priest, in the ancient belief that monarchs were sacred and ruled in God's name. For King Charles III, the oil came from olives in the Holy Land, consecrated by the Patriarch of Jerusalem and its Anglican archbishop.

Such mysticism has not always been taken seriously. Following two revolutions, the Calvinist William of Orange, one of our greatest kings, dismissed his coronation in 1689 as 'funny old popish rites'. Generations of Whigs, dissenters and the left would have agreed.

How does our literally disenchanted age respond to a golden spoon of holy oil? Many will be as dismissive as King William. Pious souls will regard it as reverently as the King himself does. Others, including me, will willingly suspend our disbelief. As Walter Bagehot put it in his classic study of the constitution, the monarchy 'consecrates our whole state'; the spoonful of oil does so literally. Consecrated by God, or by the will of the people, or by the drama of history?

Whichever we choose to believe, it renews what Edmund Burke saw as a perpetual contract between the dead, the living and the yet unborn. This imagined community of nationhood, if it is to survive and flourish, must be what the late Roger Scruton called 'the inherited first person plural' – something that over the past few years we have come perilously close to losing.

The coronation ceremony, with all its mysteries and oddities, dates back before the Norman Conquest, and it is something that we can all choose to accept and celebrate as above and beyond our present discontents. If we wish our nation to be more than 'UK plc' or a chaos of resentful factions, we should welcome the thought that at its heart is something ancient, unique, even sacred.

Notes on... Easter lilies Lara Prendergast

The Easter lily, or *Lilium longiflorum*, grows from a bulb buried underground to bear white, trumpeting flowers which face outwards and smell divine. One doesn't need to be an expert in semiotics to see why it came to be associated with the resurrection. In Christian tradition, lilies were said to have grown in the garden of Gethsemane at the spot where Jesus prayed on the eve of his crucifixion. The Easter lily is sometimes known as 'the white-robed apostle of hope'.

A few stems of lilies tied with ribbon are always a lovely present whatever the occasion, but it is true that some associate these flowers more with death than life. In depictions of the Annunciation, the angel Gabriel sometimes arrives clutching a spray of lilies. Did the Virgin Mary flinch slightly when her bouquet was delivered, laden with meaning?

The fleur-de-lis, a stylised depiction of a lily, became the official emblem of Florence in the 11th century. In Italian cities, as in much of medieval Europe, the new year used to be celebrated on 25 March, the feast day of the Annunciation, nine months before Christmas. Also known as 'Lady Day', unlike Easter, it was fixed in the calendar. In Britain, the new year began on 25 March until 1752, when our calendar changed from the Julian to the Gregorian and the dates were adjusted so that the new new year started on 5 April, which became an important feast day for accountants and tax lawyers.

Irish Republicans wear the Easter lily badge in memory of those who died during the 1916 Easter Rising. The emblem was introduced in 1926 by Cumann na mBan, the 'League of Women', and badges were sold outside church gates on Easter Sunday. Despite being known as the Easter lily, the lily depicted is in fact the Calla lily, more tubular in shape, rather than the traditional trumpet-shaped *longiflorum*.

The Easter lily itself originally hails from Taiwan and the Ryukyu Islands in southern Japan, and for much of the 19th century, lily production was based in Japan. When Pearl Harbor was attacked in 1941, the supply of bulbs from Japan stopped and Easter lilies became far more expensive to source in America. The market soon adjusted, with production shifting to a small area on the Oregon-California border, now known as the Easter lily capital of the world. Almost 95 per cent of the world's Easter lilies are still grown in this region, with five farms owned by four families producing 14 million a year. Locals refer to the flower as 'white gold'.

Enthusiasts buy their potted Easter lilies early, ideally on the Monday of Easter week to give the flowers time to open. Pollen is hell to get out of clothes so it's sensible to remove the stamens as soon as they are visible. If pollen does brush against clothes, do not try to use water to remove the yellow dust. It will only set the stain. Instead, use a piece of Sellotape to lift it off.

Some churches will ask for donations for Easter lilies in memoriam of loved ones. Potted Easter lilies can be replanted for the following year, which continues the theme of resurrection. But if cut lilies are past their best, there is nothing to be done but recognise the fact that death follows life. As Shakespeare wrote: 'For sweetest things turn sourest by their deeds; Lilies that fester smell far worse than weeds.'

Notes on... Toffee apples Tanya Gold

Bonfire night is more about burning Catholics than haute cuisine and it shows. I've always felt for Catholic friends at this time of year, but I am a Jew, and I am told I am oversensitive. It's also three decades since I made £150 doing 'Penny for the Guy' on Hampstead High Street. The last time I went to a bonfire night party it was hosted by a Catholic, and this confused me, until I remembered: she is an *English* Catholic.

If Christmas is for the goose, and Easter for the hot cross bun, bonfire night has the toffee apple. Because this is a desolate festival, it has neither toffee on the apple – we will get to that – nor, too often, a bonfire. I'm not for burning Guido in effigy like those pyromaniac loons in Lewes, about whom I always think: who will they burn next? But if I go to bonfire night, I want a bonfire, and they are often cancelled because they are dangerous, which is the

SORRY I JUST HATE TOFFEE APPLES!

point of them, and a bonfire night without a bonfire is a Christmas without Christ. The toffee apple suits its festival: you need fire to make it.

As with most famous dishes, the origin of the toffee apple is contested (not as much as better foods, but still). Honey and sugar were used as preservatives in ancient times, and it's not impossible that sugar was heated to coat the apple. But I like to think wise ancients were more careful of their teeth: a toffee apple can steal a molar and laugh. It's likely the Victorians knew how to make them, and I found a food blogger who called them a Russian delicacy.

We know this: in 1908, a confectioner called William W. Kolb of Newark, New Jersey, made a series of bright red sugared apples with cinnamon for his Christmas window display. These are candy apples, not toffee apples – you need butter or cream to make toffee. Even so, people liked them. Like Cassandras predicting late-stage capitalism, widespread morbid obesity and misnaming common things, they ate the window display. If this story is true, the toffee apple is an accidental food like the Caesar salad, which was invented in Mexico when a chef had a panic attack. It is also not a toffee apple. It is a candy apple.

Now they are everywhere in autumn, when apples are plentiful. Purists make caramel apples, which are really toffee apples, because they contain butter, or cream. Hunter's Candy in Moscow, Idaho, sold them from 1936 but, as with the toffee apple that should be called a candy apple, it is likely that they existed earlier. There are variations wherever you find apples: you can add chocolate or nuts and if you are grandiose you can paint them. They were sent to the front in the second world war, alongside salami.

But the caramel apple isn't the same. Not enough sugar. You want the crack of the sugar, and the sourness of a Granny Smith. A sweet apple cannot be a toffee apple. It makes no sense. Nor can a waxed apple. The sugar slides off. Nor can a soft apple, which collapses. If you make your own, beware. For a toffee apple, the sugar must be heated to 140°C for the desired 'hard crack'. This is a dangerous foodstuff for frightened nights, and that's apt.

Notes on... Cocaine **Julie Burchill**

It always amuses me in January to observe the fuss people make about quitting booze for a month. Because a few years ago, after three decades of taking cocaine on a daily basis, I gave it up overnight. Over-eating, gambling, shopping, pornography – there's no cheap thrill that can't be mastered with a little self-control.

I first took cocaine as a teenager working at the *New Musical Express*. As someone who had presented herself as a fearless punk when she was actually a shy virgin, I was already a big fan of the amphetamine sulphate, so when a man from a major record label said 'May I?' and starting racking out lines on my desk one day I was anticipating the familiar burn of baby laxative with the merest soupçon of speed. Imagine my horror when I experienced something far more pleasant! Instead of the desire to argue about whether the Sex Pistols were better than The Clash, I wanted to give the world a hug.

I soon found myself in the eye of the maelstrom that was the 1980s London media, making mad money and spending it on that thing you spend it on when you've got too much money. Ironically, the effects of speed and cocaine are very similar. But the reason cocaine is more expensive is because you pay for what you don't get; the crash landing is softer. It's the party drug *par excellence* in that it keeps you going. It kept my party going. And then, I'd simply had enough. You hear so much rubbish about Cold Turkey Cocaine Hell. Compare that to Keith Richards talking to *Rolling Stone* magazine on why he quit drinking. 'It's been about a year now… I got fed up with it… It was time to quit, just like all the other stuff.'

At the risk of bringing the party down, there's a serious reason why I gave up. Cocaine is like pornography; everyone wants to believe that regardless of the misery and broken lives which litter the production of everybody else's kicks, the source we alone opt for is magically free of exploitation, torture and death. In my day we kidded ourselves that growing the coca plant gave the farmers of South America a good living, which was pathetically self-deluding enough, but it's always easier to lie to ourselves about the plight of people in faraway countries of which we know nothing. Today, it would be an actual moral cretin who could ignore the human collateral which is left lying in the wake of the 'cheeky' line of coke which brings a sparkle to the eye of the after-dinner educated.

The NHS once published a guide to assist the 'very young' children being recruited in their thousands by the drug-running County Lines gangs and whose admittance to hospital with knife injuries doubled in three years. 'Clean-eaters on coke' are one of our more grotesque modern types, like the humanitarian aid worker who justifies buying

sex with impoverished women because he is, after all, one of the good guys. But what good is a clean gut when there's blood on your hands?

I got away from cocaine without doing lasting damage to myself – but I'll never know what I did to others. That's something I'll just have to live with.

Notes on... Standing ovations Laura Freeman

'And now the end is here / And so I face the final curtain…' You said it, Frank. The lights dim, the curtain falls, exeunt all to rapturous applause. Too rapturous, if you ask me. The standing ovation, once the exception, is now the rule.

Post-Covid, I got it. After months of empty theatres and keeping the ghost lamps burning, I'd have clapped any man and his dog to the skies. But university revues, pub two-handers, primary-school plays?

I feel a scab for sitting when every man jack is on his feet. I did it at *Cabaret*, *The Glass Menagerie* and *Straight Line Crazy*. A sit-in protest. 'Grinch,' you'll say, and fair enough. But I want a standing ovation to mean something. An exclamation mark,

not just a standard full-stop. I want to save it for the best of the best.

The critic Fiona Mountford, a woman who has seen more plays than you've had hot pre-theatre dinners, once gave me a piece of advice about star ratings. She said that while you might wrestle with your conscience over a three- or four-star review, with a five-star show you just knew. The same goes for standing ovations. The rise should be unbidden, your clutch bag slipping off your lap as you stand. Bravo! Brava! Bravissima! At *Jerusalem*, my husband turned to me and whispered: 'Standing?' I was already halfway up. At *Frozen the Musical*, I stood, I whooped, I cried 'Encore!' No luck. The show must not go on. Most of the audience, average age seven, were past their bedtime.

If you stand for every clog dance, what are you going to do when Vadim Muntagirov pulls off a perfect solo from *La Bayadère*? A dancer's curtain-call curtsey is called a 'révérence'. It is performed at the end of classes to thank the teacher and in front of the red curtains to thank the black-tied stalls.

I'll never forget the night I went to the Bolshoi. The bouquets of flowers brought on at the end, then picnic hampers of flowers, Alibaba baskets of flowers, Moses baskets of flowers. Finally, Roman Abramovich was ushered on stage, like a prize orchid, to kiss the prima ballerina. I saw Zenaida Yanowsky's swan-song as principal dancer for the Royal Ballet in 2017, dancing the lead in Frederick Ashton's *Marguerite* and *Armand*. The curtain call must have lasted half an hour. It was ecstatic, euphoric and endless. I was desperate for a wee.

When an actor or a company milks it, I always think of Fräulein Schweiger, first soloist of the choir of St Agatha's Church, who in *The Sound of Music* wins fourth place in the Salzburg Musical Festival and bows so much and so often that she has to be ushered off the stage. Don't be a Schweiger. Leave them hungry. That's all, folks.

Andrew Lloyd Webber and lyricist Charles Hart got it right in *The Phantom of the Opera*. When leading lady Carlotta refuses to take the stage, for the understandable reason that cast and crew keep dying in gruesome circumstances, she persuades herself back with the promise of the curtain call. In her dressing room she sings to her own reflection: 'Think how you'll shine/ In that final encore!/ Sing, prima donna, once more!'

Notes on... Rats Jon Day

In the ranks of unloved animals, rats are surely king – so reviled that other pest species are often referred to as variations of the rat archetype: pigeons are 'rats with wings', grey squirrels are 'tree rats'. In 2023 there was a flurry of tabloid stories about Britain facing an 'invasion' of '300 million monstrous super-rats capable of gnawing on steel and chewing through concrete'.

Yet how reliable were these stories? The 300 million figure is from Steven Belmain, a Greenwich University professor, who was simply giving his estimate of the rat population. (Probably an underestimate, he says, but there has never been a proper survey.) Nor is there any evidence that our rats are changing in size or nature. It's been known for some time that they're increasingly resistant to poison, but the bigger problem for the pest control industry is that poison may be banned anyway, due to concerns about it spreading into our water and food chains.

Such hysteria is the latest instalment in a long history of rat-bashing that owes much to the creature's ubiquity. The UK's most common species is the brown rat, *Rattus norvegicus*, which first came here from

China, most likely as a stowaway on ships. (The Latin name is a misapprehension – when the species was formally recorded by the 18th-century English naturalist John Berkenhout, there were no brown rats in Norway.) Around the time of the Normans it was joined by its smaller cousin, the black or 'ship' rat, *Rattus rattus*, but this is now something of a rarity. Since its migration, the brown rat has flourished, colonising cities in particular, where it lives in our sewers, under our floorboards and sometimes in our cavity walls.

It is because of this proximity that rats are so hated. But we shouldn't ignore the vast sacrifices they have made in the history of human flourishing. Rats are one of the most common animal subjects for scientific testing. Most of the world's lab rats are descendants of a single individual: the 'Wistar rat', a docile albino strain bred at the Wistar institute in Pennsylvania in 1906. Other, more unfortunate offspring include the 'spontaneously hypertensive rat' (bred to have high blood pressure), the 'BioBreeding rat' (which spontaneously develops Type 1 diabetes) and the 'Royal College of Surgeons rat' (which suffers from retinal degeneration).

Rats have also occasionally been used as a food source. Rat pie was a popular dish in Victorian Britain, and a recipe for 'grilled rats, Bordeaux style' required the use of 'alcoholic rats, found in wine cellars'. During rationing in the second world war, British biologists developed a recipe for 'creamed lab rat'. What it tasted like goes unrecorded.

Despite this utility, rats have always been reviled. The myths surrounding them are alarming, but often unfounded. Recent studies have shown it was humans rather than rats – or even their fleas – who were the principal vectors of the black death. Though they carry some unpleasant diseases (Weil's, in particular), so do many other wild animals.

We don't really hate rats because they are vermin, or carry disease or damage property. We hate them because they remind us too much of ourselves.

Notes on... Tabletop games Gus Carter

Warhammer is a tabletop battle game. Players build and paint little models of aliens, tanks and killer robots and then set their armies against one another on a miniature battlefield. It's a hobby that lights up the obsessive bits of the male brain: collecting, DIY, military uniforms, hierarchy and complex calculation – all in the name of domination. There are Warhammer clubs across the country as well as 138 dedicated Games Workshops where players can battle one another. Enthusiasts have long been stigmatised as hygienically challenged young men with limited knowledge of the opposite sex; that's certainly how I remember my early teens when I was – briefly – into Warhammer. According to Rick Priestley, its inventor, his game is seen as 'something done in secret by young men'.

But perhaps its adherents are more varied than I'd suspected. It turns out the former Foreign Secretary, Sir James Cleverly, is a fan. His private YouTube channel is dedicated to following expert miniatures painters. In 2012, he tweeted out a video on how to paint Astorath the Grim, high chaplain of the Blood Angels Space Marine Chapter.

Tabletop war games were first thought up in Prussia in the early 19th century as an alternative to chess for armchair generals. Different units were given numerical values to determine their attacking strengths and defensive weaknesses while dice were used to determine probability of success during play. In the 1820s, the Prussian general staff was presented with Kriegsspiel, designed using the latest information from the front line. By royal decree, copies of the game were bought for every regiment and officers were ordered to play it regularly.

Prussian success during the Napoleonic wars has been attributed to their tradition of wargaming. A 2019 US Naval College study found that 'Prussian forces were more often than not outnumbered, weapon advantages were mixed, and training methods were similar' but 'wargaming appears to have provided a significant advantage'.

H.G. Wells became obsessed with war games when his friend Jerome K. Jerome began firing a miniature canon at tin soldiers after what must have been a particularly raucous dinner. Wells developed his own larger version of Kriegsspiel in his book *Little Wars: a game for boys from twelve years of age to one hundred and fifty and for that more intelligent sort of girl who likes boys' games and books* (to give it its full title), detailing rules on logistics and the transportation of troops. His adherents included the actor Peter Cushing, who had an army of around 5,000 figurines and would spend up to nine hours running Wells's battle games.

In the late 1970s, a small group of wargame obsessives in Nottingham managed to get the UK import rights for Dungeons and Dragons, a fantasy tabletop game. When the licence ran out, they needed an alternative source of income. Their miniatures company Games Workshop launched Warhammer in 1983, growing from a mail order operation run out of a spare bedroom to a FTSE 250 company. Nottingham has now become a place of pilgrimage for nerds across the globe. Americans who want to visit the many toy foundries in the town, as well as Warhammer World, can spend $5,699 on a specially devised two-week tour. Perhaps they'll find Sir James there, too.

Notes on... Confetti Melanie McDonagh

All things considered, probably the least of George Osborne's concerns on the occasion of his second marriage was being showered with orange confetti by a woman apparently sympathetic to the Just Stop Oil protestors. Bingo: in the summer of 2023, a whole new form of protest came into being.

What is the whole confetti thing about anyway? You used to be able to tell if there'd been a wedding at a church by the amount of pastel-coloured horseshoe and bell shapes ground into the pavement outside. It was sold in boxes decorated with wedding motifs. Nowadays, no eco-chic guest would throw paper confetti; dried flower petals are the way to go, available in tasteful cones and a useful way of recycling dead flowers. (Really, the protestor should just have thrown marigolds.) The Victorians might have lobbed rice instead.

The roots of the custom lie with the Romans, and probably further back, with the *sparsiones*, or shower, that was customary at funerals as well as weddings. But in that case stuff was thrown at the crowd by the happy couple as well as at them.

Virgil, in his 'Eclogues', tells bridegrooms to 'scatter nuts', which he meant literally. Hugh Nibley observed in the *Classical Journal* that 'bride and groom could no more evade the obligation of scattering presents to the populace than they could avoid the meal [grains] that the populace threw at them'. Among the things people might scramble for were bits of hawthorn branches for luck – think of the throwing of the bride's bouquet today. And grains or beans signified fertility.

It's all designed to mark a wedding as a public event, something for everyone to share in. Not much different then from the Italian wedding described in Charles Dickens's journal *Household Words*, where: 'The bride appeared; there was a merry shout. The bridegroom followed with his friends, and instantly he and his friends began to throw, over the bride's head, among the assembled folk a storm of comfits [sweets]. Woe to the bridegroom who is mean on such occasions, and economises in his dealings with the comfit merchant! No sweetmeats, no acclamation – for such is the custom of the country.' The comfits might have been sugared coriander seeds.

Paper confetti goes back to 1875, when an Italian businessman, Enrico Mangili, began selling it for use in Milan's annual carnival. Before that the participants in the parade might bombard the crowd with sweets; the crowd might say it with eggs or mud. Milan being a centre of silk manufacture, Mangili began collecting the small paper discs from the punched sheets used by the silkworm breeders as bedding, and sold them for throwing. The product took off for weddings.

Moving from solid items to paper or petal confetti was safer as well as cheaper. In 1820, William Gunter, an English confectioner visiting Italy, observed in his *Confectioner's Oracle*: 'They pleasantly pelt each other with these trifles. But an English country gentleman threw his comfits with such savagery that he actually put out one of the eyes of his young bride!' George got off lightly.

Notes on... Pebble-spotting Laura Freeman

P-p-pick up a pebble. Feel its weight in your palm. Roll it over under your thumb. Any good? Not sure? Shuck it back on the shingle. Plenty of fish in the sea and more pebbles still on the shore.

In *The Pebbles on the Beach: A Spotter's Guide*, Clarence Ellis, pebble-spotter par excellence, opens with the words: 'Most people collect something or other: stamps, butterflies, beetles, moths, dried and pressed

BARBARA HEPWORTH

wildflowers, old snuffboxes, china dogs and so forth. A few eccentrics even collect bus tickets! But collectors of pebbles are rare.' We are not talking about the common or garden or indeed communal garden collector of pebbles – the sort with a wheelbarrow and a trowel. A true pebble-spotter does not make off with cartloads to resurface the driveway. 'Let us hasten to add,' Mr Ellis hastens to add, 'that we mean discriminating collectors.'

Men such as Jim Ede, founder of Kettle's Yard in Cambridge, who made his house a home for modern art, sculpture and pebbles. 'The Louvre of the Pebble,' the poet Ian Hamilton Finlay called it. Ede was particular about pebbles. 'You find a perfect pebble once in a generation,' he proclaimed. At Kettle's Yard he assembled a spiral of nearly perfectly spherical pebbles. When a friend of a friend sent him a pebble she thought would do, he sent his regrets: 'Mighty kind,' but 'I'm an awfully difficult pebble fiend'. The pleasure wasn't in the possession so much as the spotting, the stooping, the picking up, the polishing with a pocket handkerchief.

In the introduction to his biography of Augustus John, Michael Holroyd raises the question of 'invasion' – the ways a subject gets under a biographer's skin. While writing a biography of *Ede, Ways of Life: Jim Ede and the Kettle's Yard Artists*, I became a pebble fiend and an awfully difficult one at that. And so, when we find ourselves on the coast and my husband looks out to the far horizon and breathes the salty air and says 'Just look at that sea!', I grunt and go back to squinting at the beach beneath my feet.

Barbara Hepworth and Henry Moore did their best to better pebbles with their sculpture, knowing it was a game that they could only lose. 'Many people select a stone or a pebble to carry for the day,' said Hepworth. 'The weight and form and texture felt in our hands relates us to the past and gives us a sense of a universal force. The beautifully shaped stone washed up by the sea is a symbol of continuity, a silent image of our desire for survival, peace or security.' Or just a summer holiday souvenir. Whitstable – 2014. Hastings – 2017. Mousehole – 2023.

If you're lucky, you might find a hag stone: a pebble with a hole worn through it, otherwise known as an adder stone and thought to ward off nightmares, witches and snakebites. A friend finds carnelians on his nearest stretch of Norfolk sand. 'Best,' he says, 'on a sunny winter's day, You need low light to catch the translucence'. But let's stop there. We are not lapidaries, nor are we panning for gold. We are pebble-spotters, plain and simple. But there is no prize so precious or semi-precious as a practically perfect pebble picked up on a public beach.

53

Notes on... Gilets Henry Jefferys

I recently attended a summer reunion at my prep school. The occasion was the leaving of a much-loved master. I thought that the appropriate thing to wear would be a tweed jacket in honour of prep-school masters everywhere. I found myself woefully overdressed. Pretty much all of my contemporaries were wearing gilets. It was a similar story this year at the Fortnum & Mason awards, the Oscars of the British food and drink scene. I wore a suit, but it seemed as if every other guest was casually sporting a gilet.

When I was growing up the only people who wore gilets were fishermen, farmers and Michael J. Fox in *Back to the Future*. Furthermore, they weren't called gilets, they were called body warmers or sleeveless coats. Gilet is a French word, though it has very different connotations there thanks to the antics of *les gilets jaunes*.

The gilet has completely taken over the wine world. The modern wine man no longer goes for a tweed jacket and red trousers. He wears jeans, a gilet, preferably emblazoned with the name of a producer, and brown leather boots for tramping around vineyards. I think part of the reason why English wine producers, especially ex-City boys, love a gilet so much is that it suggests the wearer is more involved with the agricultural side of the business than he really is. A gilet says that the wearer is equally at home in the boardroom and the fields. It's the same affectation as driving a Range Rover in Kensington.

Perhaps the apotheosis of this style is Charlie Ireland, the adviser from *Clarkson's Farm*. Whether he's in the office or out in the fields discussing crop yield, he is rarely without a green sleeveless fleece with smart leather piping. If you want to ape his look, only one brand will do: Schöffel. This Bavarian company has become so popular that its £150 gilets are known as Cotswolds/Chelsea (delete as appropriate) life jackets. Though a Lincolnshire gentleman farmer tells me: 'Schöffel is done. Strictly for trainee land agents.' Instead he recommends getting something in Donegal tweed from Magee 1886. Yours for around £250.

You can spend a lot more. Net-a-Porter will sell you gilets from Brunello Cucinelli for up to £4,000. Gilets are also the kind of stealth luxury item that's massively popular with businesses looking to plant their logos, replacing the 1990s golfing umbrella as the branded merch of choice. Rocking a hedge-fund gilet at the school sports day is a great way of saying, I am casual and raking it in.

As you might have guessed, I am something of a gilet-sceptic. Or I was until a couple of years ago, when I went on a press trip to a distillery in Scotland and we were each issued with a branded fleece-lined gilet. I have to admit it was a revelation: snugly warm when you zip it up, but not claustrophobic, flattering on my middle-aged frame and full of handy pockets. Truly it's the perfect item for weather. Just not to parties, please. Have some standards.

Notes on... Valentine's Day Freddy Gray

One of the many things I love about my wife is that she doesn't make me do anything for Valentine's Day. Bloody Valentine's. It brings nothing but resentment and misery. It makes single people feel left out and lonely and turns happy couples against each other. True, some women might feel a little gratified if their man buys them expensive flowers – particularly if the florist delivers to her office so that others can see just how special she is. She might also enjoy being taken out for an expensive meal at a restaurant full of other couples making each other feel special on this special day.

'Darling, I had to book four months in advance coz they get so busy.'

'Darling, I can see!'

We all know such thrills are fleeting and vain. They only lead to bitterness if they are not bettered each year, on the next 14 February, in perpetuity. People who take

these occasions seriously should not be taken seriously.

Do you think me a curmudgeon? I don't think I am, necessarily, and I don't think my wife secretly pines for some over-the-top romantic gesture because the supermarkets and the television tell her that's what should happen.

It feels like a cliché to say that Valentine's is infantile or materialistic. But what else should we call it? Any semblance of romance or real sweetness is wiped out each year amid a consumerist blizzard.

In my inbox I can see an email: 'Most Luxurious Valentine's Gift: Turn the lights down at W South Beach'. It's an advertisement for an 'exclusive three-night package' holiday in Miami, including 'helicopter transportation, a Ferrari car loaner, seaplane tour, private yacht excursion, penthouse accommodations, and aphrodisiac-inspired in-room dining with a menu curated by The Dutch's Chef Andrew Carmellini'. Classy – and all yours for $55,000.

'This is really one of the most luxurious Valentine's Gift [sic] money *can* buy.' Who would give that sort of money to a company that puts so little effort into their basic pitch?

At the other end of the scale, I've been sent a Valentine's message from Asda. 'Can you feel the love tonight?' it says.

The answer is no.

Asda are offering, among other treats, a heart-shaped egg-shaper ('egg-stra special'), cupcake makers ('Show off your sweet side'), heart-shaped tea lights ('Show your love heart your sweeter side'), some bottles of bubble mixture ('Treat your love bird').

It's all so weirdly unthinking and childish: as if they were flogging candy to babies, which in a way they are, because the only people really interested in Valentine's are teenagers, too young to realise that their incipient sentimentality is being exploited by marketing departments. Oh, and morons with more money than sense. Everybody else thinks Valentine's Day is ghastly, and so they should.

Notes on... Elderflower Flora Watkins

There's an old saying that English summertime begins when the frothy heads of elderflowers appear in hedgerows – and ends when the black elderberries have ripened. People have been picking these great white 'plates', as the flower heads are known, to make drinks since at least Tudor times. In Hannah Glasse's *The Art of Cookery Made Plain and Easy* (1747) there's a recipe for elderflower wine. But only in

the past 20 years or so have elderflower cordial and pressé become ubiquitous as soft drinks.

That expansion has largely been brought about by Peverel Manners of Belvoir Fruit Farms in Leicestershire. 'Pev', a cousin of the Duke of Rutland, still uses his mother's recipe. Lady Mary Manners got it from Lady Astor while staying at Cliveden, where it was always on the drinks tray. In 1984 Lady Mary started commercial production with 100 cases. The elderflowers were picked by three carloads of local children, driven around the Vale of Belvoir by Pev and his parents. Last year some ten million bottles of Belvoir's elderflower cordial were sold worldwide. At weddings and parties, it's no longer acceptable to be offered Britvic or Coke if you're not drinking, and Pev is proud to have 'built a whole new category of adult soft drinks'. Other brands abound, but he points out that most use elderflower extract rather than the real thing.

Today it takes more than a few local kids to gather the 50,000 tons needed to meet the global demand. Belvoir now promotes the elderflower harvest as a family day out, with influencers invited to Instagram the blossoms. Pickers are paid £3 a kilo, with the most industrious gathering up to 50 kg a day. It is a middle-class version of the Cockney hop-pickers' annual Kentish holiday.

The elder is a curious tree, steeped in myth. It's tricky to cultivate, preferring hedgerows and hidden glades, although it also grows prolifically in London parks. Elderflower is best picked on sunny days when the sprays are full of the heady yellow pollen that gives the drink its flavour. Don't pick them if there's even a tinge of brown, however, because your cordial will smell of cat's pee.

There are four other ingredients to elderflower cordial: lemon, water, citric acid and sugar. A lot of sugar – as with marmalade, it's probably best not to know how much. Elderflower is also delicious made into jellies and cheesecakes, or cooked gently with gooseberries, with which it has a wonderful affinity. You can add a splash of the cordial to a gin and tonic, or drink as a spritzer with white wine, soda water and a leaf of borage.

The picking season starts in late May and finishes around the end of Wimbledon. But don't stand under an elder on Midsummer Night or the fairies will carry you off. And it's best to thank the goddess of the Elder Mother who lives in the tree for whatever you take. Druids held the elder sacred, while herbalists have long known its medicinal properties. The bark was used to ease the pain of childbirth and the berries to treat piles. Hot cordial will soothe a sore throat, and Pev swears elderflower cures his hay fever.

Notes on... Bagpipes Robert Porter

Many people love to hate bagpipes. Everyone from William Shakespeare to Alfred Hitchcock has held them in contempt. For some, they are almost a form of punishment. A few years ago, a frustrated motorist blasted bagpipe music in the faces of Insulate Britain protestors on the M25 before he was stopped by police.

Most pipers will tell you they are sick of hearing that the definition of a gentleman is someone who knows how to play the bagpipes and doesn't. Equally, someone once told me the joke that the bagpipes are an ingenious breathalyser test: you blow into the bag and if the noise that comes out doesn't

CHARLIE MACPARKER 1952

want to make you kill yourself, you aren't drunk enough.

Despite bagpipes' supposed unpopularity, though, bagpiping is in its ascendancy in Britain. The Great Highland bagpipes are pre-eminent, but the Irish uilleann pipes perhaps come a close second; and then there are the Northumbrian pipes, the Scottish smallpipes, the Border pipes and the Cornish pipes, to name a few.

I play the Scottish smallpipes, which, although they have the same tunes and fingering as the Great Highland bagpipe, are reminiscent of the uilleann pipes because you 'blow' the bag with a bellows strapped to an arm rather than with a mouthpiece. Until you become sufficiently competent, this makes you look a bit like a chicken desperately trying to take off as you negotiate the bellows and bag with alternate elbows.

The repertoire that can be played on the smallpipes is vast. The usual marches, strathspeys and reels beloved of Great Highland bagpipers can be attempted, as can *piobaireachd* (known to Sassenachs as 'Scottish laments'), although many *piobaireachd* players would argue that it can only properly be played on the Great Highland bagpipe (a contention with which I disagree).

Much of the Irish uilleann piping repertoire can be adapted to the smallpipes with a little ingenuity. For instance, the beautiful slow air 'Fanny Power', by the 18th-century blind Irish harpist Turlough O'Carolan, rises to the second octave in the second part with the uilleann pipes, but a smallpipes arrangement can be devised whereby the melody modulates down to G with a satisfactory effect.

It's relatively impossible to capture the beauty of all those evocative Irish laments on the smallpipes, which is a great shame; but then the uilleann pipers do not have the beauty of the *piobaireachd* canon to fall back on.

The bagpipes have encouraged me to travel to exotic places around the globe. I've played the mysterious *piobaireachd* 'The Glen is Mine' at Concordia in Pakistan surrounded by vast peaks at the foot of K2, and 'Fanny Power' on my penny whistle as I walked in the African bush with a baby black rhino.

My ultimate piping experience was when I bungee-jumped off the Victoria Falls bridge in Zimbabwe with my pipes strapped round me as I played 'Scotland the Brave' and plummeted into the dense spray from the river below. It was good for my mental health, less so for the reeds.

Notes on… Viking words Frederick Edward

Supposedly 5 per cent of words in English are borrowed from Old Norse. It doesn't sound like a lot, but much of our key vocabulary was brought over in longboats: 'get', 'take', 'give' and 'egg' are all derived from the language of the Vikings.

Indeed, it took the Saxons centuries to *thwart* the *gangs* of *sly lads* who came across the *gusty* seas full of *anger*, hoping to *ransack* the *weak* Saxon *oafs* and *angrily hit their skulls* together.

Our Saxon *fellows* repeatedly fell victim to these *dregs* of the North Sea. They *blundered* in paying the Danegeld and only slowly learned the *awkward* lesson that this *gift* would not *get* rid of these Danish *outlaws*. By the time these *gangs staggered* back to Scandinavia, their words stayed with us, along with their settlers and settlements: any readers living in a town ending in *–by* or *–thorpe* are living somewhere founded by these marauding Norsemen.

Old Norse words didn't just replace pre-existing Anglo-Saxon ones. They supplemented the language with new words with slightly different connotations.

My favourite example of this is difference between 'slay' and 'slaughter', which despite sharing the same Proto-Indo-European roots have very different connotations. We slay the dragon, but the women and children were slaughtered. The difference is that 'slaughter' was brought over by the Vikings and adopted by the resident Anglo-Saxons to denote a touch of brutality in proceedings; presumably as the *rugged* Nordic invaders, speaking their *odd* language, *scared* the natives.

It's often forgotten that the Vikings won in the end. The Normans may have spoken French but they were descended from northmen. As a fan of Germanic languages, I wish they had kept speaking Old Norse: I much prefer the Germanic brotherliness or *Brüderlichkeit* to *fraternité*, or our freedom and *Freiheit* to the Latinate *liberté*.

That is merely personal preference, of course. Admittedly the influx of Latin words via the Normans has spared us from the German tendency to make words by gluing them together – *Unabhängigkeitserklärungen*, anyone? – but there is something pleasingly visual, almost tactile, in some of the words this process makes. Consider *schadenfreude* (*schaden* = pain, *freude* = joy), *durchfall* (literally 'through fall', aka 'diarrhoea'), and *nacktschnecke* (meaning 'naked snail', or to you and I, 'slug').

The Vikings gave us the word 'law' too and were keen on its implementation. The world's oldest surviving parliament – Iceland's Alþingi – was formed in AD 930 at Þingvellir. Modern Icelandic keeps many of the letters that the Vikings used. 'Þ' ('thorn') is pronounced 'th' and existed in English until the early Middle Ages, until it got confused with the letter 'y', leading people to believe that 'ye' is an Ye Olde version of 'the'. It isn't. It was just that the printing presses used in England were imported from the continent and didn't have a 'Þ', so they used 'y' instead.

Words mattered to the Vikings. 'Word fame' was the only consolation to be gained in their world of heroic fatalism. As the piece from the *Hávamál* – a collection of Old Norse poems – said:

'Wealth dies, kinsmen die, A man himself must likewise die; But one thing I know which never dies – The verdict on each man dead.'

Notes on... Bowls Michael Simmons

Bowls has a reputation as a sedate pastime, but it can be as fiercely competitive as any other sport. It can even get rowdy. At the Edinburgh cup final in 2012, a young player, angry at losing the match, stripped down to his boxers in protest. When committee members from his team tried to restrain him, he headbutted the club secretary.

Bowls players have always taken the sport very seriously. According to popular legend, Sir Francis Drake was playing bowls at Plymouth Hoe when the Spanish Armada came into view off the headland. He insisted on finishing the game. Battle could wait, bowls couldn't.

The object of the game is simple: get your bowls closer to the 'jack' than your opponent. That said, the sport is more sophisticated than the French variation, boules. Each bowl has a 'bias', meaning it curves to the left or the right. You can't deliver it in a straight line like a ten-pin. It's a common misconception that the bowls are weighted. In fact, they're cut at the manufacturing stage to create a high and low shoulder so they naturally bend to one side.

There are regional variations, too. In the north of England there is 'crown green', a less refined version of the game where the green isn't flat and bowlers can play in all directions. England has two rival associations with minor rule differences.

Bowls used to be made by turning wood. In the Victorian era they were often created from old railway sleepers, but nowadays they're made from a plastic resin shaped to exact specifications. One of the leading manufacturers, based in Australia, uses precision machinery originally intended for aircraft design to make sure every bowl in a set is the same.

There are many reasons to join a bowling club. Even if you're not the most able bowler, you can get your kicks by exerting political power on the volunteer committee. At my club in Edinburgh (where, at 26, I am the youngest member by at least 35 years), a yearly bone of contention is the bar prices. There's a tug of war between members, who want subsidised alcohol, and the bar convenor, who wants to beat last year's profits. Complain and you'll be hit with the question: 'Would you like to take over the role?' Invariably, no one does. The suburban dictatorship continues.

Bowls is not immune from scandal or even doping. In 2017, after winning a national championship, a team of women in their sixties was investigated by anti-doping agents. They had taken medication for high blood pressure, which turned out to be banned. Beta-blockers, another heart medication, ended up on the banned list too because the World Anti-Doping Agency thought they could help with 'shaky hands'.

The real beauty of bowls is that everyone is welcome. Working men and women, lords and ladies all mix together on the green and socialise afterwards. I've faced Downing Street special advisers, retired footballers, a lord and reformed criminals. My USP is that I'm the only club member ineligible for retiree competitions.

Notes on... The English seaside
Jenny Coad

'May I take a picture of your snake?' I asked the tattooed man with a python around his neck, regretting it as the words left my mouth. He nodded. 'What's it called?' 'There's two,' he replied, gruffly. So there were! Two pythons comfortably coiled, glistening in the sunshine.

It was the hottest early May bank holiday since the day was introduced in 1978, and the Kent coast was in full swing. The sea looked murky, the sand muddy and there was not a palm tree in sight but that did little to dent our enjoyment. You can't beat an English beach day.

On the scorching bank holiday in question, half of south London seemed to have disgorged onto Whitstable. Stalls, vans and boat clubs were doing a roaring trade in oysters, lobster rolls, pots of winkles, fried eggs in a bun, and ice cream cones.

We walked along the Saxon Shore Way. Families were settling in. Couples were sitting, eyes closed, chins up, basking in the sun. Of course everyone was going pink, in shorts, strapless dresses, off-the-shoulder tops, a mishmash. This isn't the Amalfi coast – anything goes. And it might be the only opportunity! Drink it all in. We could all do with the vitamin D.

At Herne Bay, in between queues for wood-fired pizzas and Cornettos, a businesslike woman in brilliant red clown shoes and yellow trousers was twisting purple balloons into sausage dogs for a Punch and Judy show. Had we stepped back into the 1950s?

A few children were hustled onto the mat laid out in front of the traditional tall yellow-and-red-striped theatre. But most were interested in crabbing, slinging green nets over the pier edge and winching them back up. Overhead, a purple squid kite with long fluorescent tendrils fluttered. Then the jet skis got going, roaring across the horizon.

My boyfriend, Rob, who cannot resist a stretch of water – no matter the temperature – braved a swim. He stood thigh deep for quite some time. Then he was off, quickly disappearing from view as I tried to concentrate on my book.

It took him an hour's stride back along the coast path to properly warm up again. By that time, the tide was in and the mood festive. Drinks were being poured on balconies, barbecues were smoking, plastic flutes being raised. We saw a group of runners who had passed us earlier, leaning against a wall outside the pub drinking celebratory pints. Good for them. Yes, the English seaside is barmy, but it's brilliant.

Notes on... Monopoly Andrew Watts

I've been playing a lot of Monopoly recently. My son got his first grown-up set for Christmas and, even after time has increased the entropy of his Lego sets and Scalextric, this is the present he still pulls out. I have no objection – why wouldn't I break off from completing my tax return to watch someone else squirm at income tax? – but his mother is doubtful about the game's message. She has already forbidden the card game Old Maid on feminist grounds ('You shouldn't be stigmatised for not being in a couple!'); should we really be teaching him the fun side of capitalism?

One of Fidel Castro's first actions on seizing power was to ban the game and have all sets in Cuba destroyed. The government of Hungary, less strictly doctrinaire than other communist regimes, licensed an adaptation called *Gazdálkodj Okosan!* (Budget Prudently!), which may sound joyless but had chance cards like: 'Go to the cinema! The films are instructive and entertaining. Pay ten forints.'

These communist rip-offs were in fact going back to the source. Monopoly, which was published by Parker Bros nearly a century ago, was itself adapted from The Landlord's Game, designed by American activist Elizabeth Magie to illustrate the dangers of capitalism. Her patent was later bought up by Parker Bros, just as all Monopoly players buy up properties they don't want to prevent others getting them.

The game evolved in hand-copied versions, with Magie's politics removed, but other political elements added. One version divided properties by the ethnicity of occupants; the American set's least desirable properties are still old African-American neighbourhoods.

But even in its 'capitalist' form, Monopoly doesn't celebrate capitalism. In its version of the free market, only the rent-seeking purchasers of property are free; as a player, you are compelled to go where the roll of the dice takes you. And that idea – that consumer sovereignty is an optional extra to capitalism, rather than its whole point – is a deeply unsound lesson for our children. It may teach a few valuable lessons about real estate investing – cashflow is king, and a properly diversified portfolio should not be too diversified – but that is outweighed by fantasies like buying property in Park Lane for only twice your salary. If I had any interest in banning games on political grounds, I'd ban Monopoly. The only way in which it does resemble real capitalism is that the winners think winning is a matter of skill, and the losers think it's pure luck.

Hasbro, which now owns the Monopoly monopoly, are still producing versions with different politics. There is a feminist version, featuring Ms Monopoly. Instead of real estate, players collect inventions made by women, such as space station batteries and chocolate chip cookies (although the game of Monopoly itself isn't included, despite being invented by a woman). My son is glad Father Christmas didn't give him that version – it is, apparently, stupid and unfair that girls get £240 on passing Go and boys £200 – but I might buy it for my wife.

Notes on... Pub names David Butterfield

An easy one: what links Jack Straw's Castle, The Labouring Boys and The Jolly Taxpayer? No, not the parliamentary expenses scandal of yesteryear, but the weird and whimsical world of British pub names.

It was in 1393 that Richard II ordered brewers to announce their beery business by a prominent sign. Colourful names quickly abounded, invented by publicans and patrons alike. The intervening six centuries have given ample scope for praise and play.

The commonest names across Britain's 50,000 or so pubs gesture to royal heraldry: The Red Lion, Crown, Royal Oak and White Hart make up the top four; Rose and Crown, Queen's Head and King's Arms come close behind. Most monarchs win a mention somewhere, although King Edward VIII is remembered only in The Abdication (Arnold, Notts).

Military conquests find widespread coverage, most provocatively by the Turk's, Saracen's or Black(a)moor's Head. Ye Olde Trip to Jerusalem (Nottingham) claims to have been the rallying point for the Third Crusade. But many an eponymous general, admiral or battle now falls flat with the average pubgoer. Do drinkers in The Antigallican (Charlton) still seethe with suspicion?

Traditional trades and livery companies are commemorated everywhere, with The Three Horseshoes (farriers), Masons Arms and Carpenters Arms leading the field. Mayfair's I Am the Only Running Footman preserves that livelihood's last dash. While hunting, sporting, agricultural and locomotion are ubiquitous themes, literary names are scarcer. The Rubaiyat in Glasgow closed years ago, but they're still serving at The Dr Syntax Inn (Stocksfield), The Case Is Altered (Bentley, Suffolk), The Barnaby Rudge (Tebay) and The Hobbit (Southampton).

As a rule, pub names should never change – but the occasional tweak is forgiveable. Northfield's Man in the Moon became, in 1969, the Man on the Moon; and the Bird in the Hand (Witney) became the Baby in the Hand after an emergency delivery in the car park. The oldest pub, with at least 11 centuries behind it, is the unassuming Bingley Arms in Bardsey. The highest (Tan Hill Inn, Yorkshire Dales) rises to 1,732 feet; the lowest (Admiral Wells, Peterborough) sits nine feet below sea level. The remotest (The Old Forge, Knoydart) demands an 18-mile hike or seven-mile ferry to reach a road to it.

The Kentish pubs that are the country's largest (Royal Victoria Pavilion, Ramsgate) and smallest (The Little Prince, Margate) give some advance warning of scale. And the longest pub name – The Old Thirteenth Cheshire Astley Volunteer Rifleman Corps Inn (Stalybridge) – is amusingly precise.

Here is just a taste of the riotous gallimaufry of pub names. What to make of The Drunken Duck (Ambleside), The Bucket of Blood (Phillack, Cornwall), The World Turned Upside Down (Reading), The Cardinal's Error (Tonbridge), The Honest

Politician (Portsmouth) or My Father's Moustache (Louth)? Each has a story, so sidle up to the bar and ask. But hurry: The Mother Huff Cap (Alcester), The Cow and Snuffers (Cardiff), The Sociable Plover (Portsmouth) and Who'd a Thowt It? (Middleton, Manchester) join 36,000 others that have now called time (www.closedpubs.co.uk).

Notes on… Signal boxes Christian Wolmar

Petersfield signal box is in the wrong place. Or at least it is now. When it was built in the 1880s, it was in precisely the right place, near the tracks and next to the level crossing that the signalman controlled. It had to be. Signal boxes had a series of big levers which controlled both signals and the points on the track. In the days before electric motors, the boxes had to be as near as possible to the points or shifting the levers became too difficult, especially in cold weather.

Petersfield is Grade II listed because it is a rare example of a box containing equipment developed by the London & South Western Railway, which built most of the lines out of Waterloo. It now faces demolition as Network Rail is decommissioning the box and wants to improve the level crossing next to it.

In the early days of the railway, 'policemen' had to stand next to the points to change them and were soon provided with little huts for shelter. Then, as trackwork became more complex, several points were controlled from one location and the signal box was born.

The signal box was often the local hub of the railway, frequently busier than the local station as the P-Way men (the trackworkers), the signalmen and various local people – a mix of enthusiasts and the nosy, often schoolchildren – would pop in for a chat and a cup of tea from the kettle that was always kept near to boiling on the hotplate. Keeping the box tidy and cosy was a source of great pride for the signalmen, who often spent long lonely shifts at night ensuring the smooth passage and, above all, safety of the trains they controlled. They made key decisions about which to prioritise and woe betide the one who delayed the express to allow the milk train through.

Adrian Vaughan wrote in *Signalman's Nightmare*, his account of working in eight different boxes, how in the middle of the night, his box at Challow in Oxfordshire 'looked splendid… when the red, blue, black and yellow levers with their long, brass badges and burnished steel handles flashed like a full-dress military parade under the stark light of three electric bulbs'. As the title of his book implies, Vaughan was ever worried about safety and rightly so. Britain's worst rail accident, Quintinshill, in 1915, which killed 230 people, was caused by a signalman forgetting he had routed a slow train on the path of an express.

At the time of rail nationalisation in 1948, there were more than 10,000 boxes across the network but gradually many were closed as their intricate hand-operated mechanisms were replaced by remotely operated electrics.

There are still some 700 boxes and there is hope that not all will disappear. Network Rail originally wanted to control all the signals on the network from a dozen large centres, but now, I'm told, the state-owned company will leave such decisions to regional managers. And several unused boxes have found a new life. The Railway Heritage Trust provides grants for the maintenance and upkeep of listed signal boxes and some have been moved, with their levers intact, to heritage railways where enthusiasts can play at being signallers all day long. The Petersfield signal box may survive, if not in Petersfield itself.

Notes on... Motorways Mark Mason

The first one was too straight. In the absence of a speed limit, early motorists on the M1 used the long sections without bends as racetracks. The record was set in April 1964 by two drivers testing their AC Cobra for Le Mans: they reached 185 mph. The following year new express trains appeared on the track next to the motorway, and some drivers tried to keep up with them. So the 70 mph limit was introduced. Subsequent motorways were built with curves even where they didn't need them, purely to discourage speeding.

As if driving itself wasn't risky enough, some users of the new M1 stopped for picnics on the hard shoulder, with one family even doing so on the central reservation. And when crashes happened, AA men would alert other motorists by tipping petrol on to rags, lighting them and throwing them into the road. 'When the rags had been used up,' remembered one, 'I used to throw the rest of the petrol across the motorway and set fire to it. But it didn't stop all of them – they'd go through the flames into the cars in the accident.' More recent recklessness was shown by the pranksters who, on April Fool's Day 2000, painted a zebra crossing over all three lanes of the M3 in Hampshire. The police were never quite sure how.

There's only one motorway that doesn't connect with any of the others (the M2). The longest is the M6 (232 miles), while the widest is the M25 near Heathrow (six lanes in either direction). The M62 is both the highest (1,221 feet above sea level, at the appropriately named Windy Hill in the Pennines) and the lowest (9 feet, at Goole).

Tom Robinson's 1977 hit '2-4-6-8 Motorway' was inspired by him heading home after gigs on the M1 (though the chorus is adapted from a gay liberation chant: '2-4-6-8, gay is twice as good as straight, 3-5-7-9, lesbians are mighty fine').

Motorways have other, more tangential links with culture. A stretch of the M25 appears in *Withnail and I* – the sign (visible in the background) is a continuity error, as the movie is set 20 years before the road opened. And because pulped paper is an excellent road-building material, the M6 toll motorway contains 2.5 million Mills & Boon novels.

But motorways' greatest fascination is to be found in their service stations. Rather like airports, they trap every type of person together in one place, making for a wonderful human zoo. Tebay services on the M6 have become a holiday destination in their own right, offering stunning views across Cumbria, a caravan park, hotel, duck pond and award-winning farm shop. In 2009, 73-year-old Doris Short told the *Daily Mail* how she liked to stay there, occasionally popping over to the southbound café for a coffee: 'That's a nice outing.'

London Gateway (previously known as Scratchwood) is 11.7 miles from *HMS Belfast*'s mooring on the Thames near Tower Bridge, and as this happens to be the range of the ship's guns, they're trained on the service station.

But of course the most famous stop-off remains Watford Gap. It was originally known as the Blue Boar, after the company that ran it. When Jimi Hendrix first came to Britain, he heard so many musicians talking about it that he assumed it was a nightclub.

Notes on... Brits in Paris Laura Freeman

'Yes, it's here!' says the sign above the English épicerie in Paris. 'Yes, at last,' thinks the starved expat wandering in a desert of croissants, magret de canard and monts blancs. Now for some real food: Fray Bentos pies, Quaker Oats, Fentimans lemonade, HP Sauce, Marmite, Tetley's, Twinings, Dorset cereals, Cadbury's Fruit & Nut, Altoids mints and Macsween haggis. As a sop to Americans: Pop-Tarts, Lucky Charms, Aunt Jemima's pancakes and marshmallow fluff in a jar. I know an Englishman who walks the length of the Canal Saint-Martin for proper Yorkshire Tea.

There is a Pont cartoon 'The British Character: Importance of Tea' which shows four doughty picnickers getting an oil-stove and kettle going in a gale. Never formerly a tea fusspot, in Paris I have become a Pont throwback. I face a rictus of agony when the

water comes tepid, the teabag in its wrapper and the milk UHT. One cannot stay cheerful on plongeur's dishwater. Carette on the Place des Vosges and Le Fumoir opposite the Louvre do loose leaves and cold milk.

The Louvre's gallery of British art is the furthest feather of the Denon wing. Miles of enfilading Spaniards and Italians, then in the last room: a holy trinity of Constable, Gainsborough, Turner (the only Turner in a French public collection) lumped in with the Yanks. The frame of Gainsborough's Lady Alston was meant for a portrait of Madame de Pompadour: she wears it well. Thomas Lawrence's 'The Children of John Julius Angerstein' hangs next to Richard Dadd's 'Titania Sleeping'. Is Mad Dadd the best we can do?

If you're pining for the Wallace Collection, the Musée Jacquemart-André is small and sumptuous. Here, for the patriotic, is Paolo Uccello's Saint George 'Slaying the Dragon'. In the National Gallery's version, painted ten years later, the dragon is more marauding, but the Jacquemart-André's dragon with his arthritic knees has charm.

When you feel you will scream if you see another mimsy garden of box-hedges and curated gravel, take the train to Chantilly. The chateau's painting collection is stupidly gorgeous – you go round goggling – and the gardens, once you get away from Le Notre, better than Blenheim.

My friend the foreign correspondent claims Shakespeare & Co. sells 10,000 copies of Hemingway's *A Moveable Feast* each year. Nice fact if it's true. The Shakespeare & Co. you see now isn't the one Sylvia Beach opened in 1919 as a bookshop and hangout for Hemingway, Joyce, Pound and Scott Fitzgerald. Beach, who helped publish Joyce's *Ulysses*, was saddened to see the book listed in catalogues of erotica with *Fanny Hill* and *Casanova*. An Irish priest, buying *Ulysses*, once asked her: 'Any other spicy books?' Spicy or sweet, the shop is stocked to the rafters. Selfies are banned.

L'Entente, the British brasserie, opened in 2018. It has defied the sniggering and on a weekday is full of Parisians eating Welsh rarebit with Lea & Perrins Worcestershire sauce. The shepherd's pie with homemade ketchup is le business. The bill comes with Brighton rock.

If none of that works, and you're still crawling-the-walls homesick, you can be home, depending on proximity to St Pancras, door-to-door in five hours. Four-and-a-half at a hustle.

Notes on... The Bank of England   Mark Mason

'Safe as the Bank of England.' So goes the old phrase. And yes, with walls 8ft thick, the Old Lady is pretty impregnable. Even the keys to her vaults are more than a foot long (the locks also now incorporate voice-activated software). Until 1973 the building was guarded at night by soldiers from the Brigade of Guards, who received a pint of beer with their dinner there. With all this security, how can you hope to get in?

One answer came in 1836, when the directors received an anonymous letter inviting them to meet the letter writer in the bullion room late one night. At the agreed hour they heard some floorboards being dislodged, and looked down to see a man's head appearing. He worked in the sewers, and had calculated that a drain ran directly underneath the vault. The Bank rewarded him £800 – worth around 80 grand today, but still not as much as he could have got by nicking all the gold. That's the gold, by the way, that can only be stacked six pallets high – otherwise it would sink into the clay bedrock on which the Bank is built.

Best to assume this drain has been blocked, so what are your options? Every autumn there's Open House, the weekend when famous London buildings welcome public visitors. I went during Mervyn King's governorship. On his desk sat a cricket ball with which he'd taken five wickets for the Bank. (Sadly 'Merv the Swerve' was a spinner rather than a swing bowler.) Or you could visit the wonderful museum in the Bank's south-east corner (open Monday to Friday, free entry). There are old white fivers, a real gold bar – you have to try and pick it up with one hand – and a signed first edition of *The Wind in the Willows*, whose author Kenneth Grahame worked at the Bank for 30 years.

But this is tourist stuff. What about the working part of the Bank – how can you get in there? Someone once told me you're allowed in to exchange damaged banknotes. So when my dog chewed a tenner, off I went, presenting myself at the main entrance on Threadneedle Street. 'Very sorry, sir,' said the doorman. 'You do that by post these days.' The form was interesting. 'How did the damage occur?' 'Eaten by dog.' 'Where is the missing portion of the note?' 'Inside dog.' Even though by then it probably wasn't.

Then I heard that though damaged notes are dealt with by post, old notes (in other words ones that are no longer legal tender) are replaced on the premises. Clearing out my partner's father's house after he died, we found a fiver from the 1980s. Again I made the trip, bracing myself for more disappointment.

This time the bastion fell. 'Certainly, sir. Just through there.' Quick bag search inside the front door, make a right and you're into a room that looks just like a normal bank (Perspex screens and all), albeit with impressive paintings of previous Governors on the walls. Indeed until last year Bank employees could use this room as a normal bank: their accounts bore the cherished sortcode 10-00-00. One of the three tellers examined my fiver (available on eBay for not much more than face value, should you wish to enjoy the experience yourself), then issued me with a replacement. Safe.

Notes on... Ruins   Harry Mount

We're so used to looking at the abbeys smashed up by Henry VIII that we forget quite how odd they are.

It's not just that they've been preserved as ruins for 500 years, although that's odd enough in a country that's only saved ruins properly for a century. What's odder is that these vast structures were built in such remote spots. It's like finding a ruined Westminster Abbey in the middle of nowhere. When the Cistercians left Clairvaux in Burgundy, they were so desperate for peace that they came all the way north to found Rievaulx in 1132, and Byland a few years later.

For 400 years, before the abbeys were smashed, they were the biggest buildings for miles, with vast flocks of monks and lay brothers. And yet the valleys around remained deserted. Today, Byland and Rievaulx are still tiny settlements. I lay in the evening sun and stared at Rievaulx's ruins for an hour without hearing a single car. Only the swifts and pigeons broke the silence. No mobile signal either – irritating when you want to muck about on the internet; heaven when you're channelling Cistercian calm.

We had Rievaulx to ourselves that evening because we were staying in the old caretaker's cottage, built out of the ruined abbey's stone, which gives you access to the abbey after closing. That emptiness is a gift in the busy summer season; even busier, now there's a visitors' centre and a small stylish museum. The museum's star feature is a 13th-century Christ in Majesty sculpture, his head chopped off by iconoclasts, leaving a decapitated Christ in a crisply carved belted gown. The Abbey Inn in Byland – also built out of the abbey's stone – doesn't offer after-hours access to the ruins. But the Mouseman bedroom does give a head-on view of the great butchered half-circle of Byland's rose window. Once again, I stared and stared.

Why are ruins so hypnotic? The conventional wisdom is that the joy of ruins is a human construct, created by Sir John Vanbrugh when he tried to preserve the ruins of Woodstock Manor as a charming eye-catcher at Blenheim Palace. That silly old modernist, the Duchess of Marlborough, ignored him and knocked it down in 1720.

I'm not sure the conventional wisdom is right. There's an innate pleasure in seeing pure blue sky through Rievaulx's empty windows, once filled with mullions, transoms and glass. There's a thrilling horror at Henry VIII's monstrosity when you see Rievaulx's fother – a chunk of lead, shaped like a mammoth bar of soap, formed from the abbey's melted roof. The fire to melt the lead was fed by burning medieval choir stalls. And there's a pleasing game in filling the ruins' gaps by extrapolating from the fragments. At Byland, you can still see bits of the monks' stone choir stalls, and the partitioned corners of the cloisters where they illuminated their manuscripts. Suddenly, the ghosts of medieval England are heart-stoppingly close.

Notes on... Ice cream Laura Freeman

It was a mistake to tell us about the gelati-to-sightseeing ratio. This was the formula my father, his younger sister and brother came up with when being dragged round Italian churches as children. The ideal was 3:1, that is: three ice creams for each dreary *chiesa*. My grandparents thought it should be the other way around: three improving historic sights for every one ice cream.

Of course, once my brother and I knew about the gelati ratio – and what an astonishing thought it was that our father had once been young and had sat mutinous on the steps of the Parthenon – we knew not to be fobbed off with one lousy scoop of choc chip. We wanted a 1:1 ratio or bust. In England, slopping around the Lost Gardens of Heligan in wellies and waterproofs, we settled for hot chocolates. But on rare spring and summer days and on holiday, it was Twisters, Viennettas and three scoops of Neapolitan in glass bowls.

Outside our primary school in the summer term, an ice-cream van used to park on the hill, bonnet towards the Finchley Road. The jingle started at three minutes to four, wildly distracting to seven-year-olds doing times tables. Now when I hear an ice cream van playing 'The Entertainer' rag it gives me a craving – more slaveringly Pavlovian than Proustian – for a mint Cornetto, the paper peeled off in a neat helix. In the holidays we were allowed to buy Mini Milks from the corner shop, a trip that could be taken On Our Own, crossing two roads, with 20ps folded in our palms. Mini Milks taste of first London freedoms and pocket money to burn.

Ice creams do taste of freedom: long summer evenings and layers shed and sunburnt holidays and sod-the-calories. On my graduation day, broiling in black dress, black tights, black gown and fur hood in a June heatwave, my university boyfriend and I had Calippos by the river. The orange syrup promised a sunny future, the world at our feet, never an exam again. The relationship melted, as ice lollies and university boyfriends do, but a Calippo remains a sticky symbol of great happiness.

My tastes are more acid now: bitter blood-orange sorbets rather than sickly Twisters. Earlier this year at Le Querce, an Italian restaurant in south London recommended by fellow I-scream-you-scream-we-all-scream-for-ice-cream friends, I was ready to order the rapa rossa (beetroot) sorbet when the patron came to the table wearing an expression of deep grief, as if the family's beloved nonna, who had first taught them to beat cream with vanilla, had just died.

There had been a terrible accident, he said, a fault with the freezer overnight: the kitchen's stock of gelati – myrtle berry and pear, pumpkin and amaretto – had turned to slush. But all was not lost. He had had time to whip up just one batch of banana, cardamom and ginger. And so we had that, with long silver spoons, on the first April evening mild enough to be out without a coat, and a heady sense of summer just beyond the next bus stop.

Notes on... Soho drinking clubs   Henry Jefferys

When someone says 'Let's go for a drink at my club', what do you imagine? A grand St James's establishment like Boodle's or White's, or perhaps a media hangout such as the Groucho or Soho House? What you probably don't think of is an unmarked door and a flight of rickety stairs. Yet through unpromising-looking doorways in and around Soho are little clubs where you can take a break from the 21st century. Places such as the Phoenix beneath the Phoenix theatre on Charing Cross Road, Gerry's on Dean Street and the Academy on Lexington Street are relics of a time (Gerry's has been going since 1955) when pubs had to close after lunch and not open again until the evening. People needed somewhere to drink in the afternoon and after 11 p.m. last orders. These clubs met the demand.

They are subtly different from places like the Groucho, where the successful and the ambitious congregate to sell things to each other. Nobody ever got any work done at Gerry's. Chris Evans won't be at the next table at the Phoenix. Not that you won't run into celebrities – they'll just be of the loucher sort. At the artist Sebastian Horsley's 40th birthday at the Colony Room, I found myself drinking alongside Shane MacGowan and Bryan Ferry. A friend reminisced about hearing David Soul of *Starsky & Hutch* fame belting out his hit 'Silver Lady' at Gerry's one night. The Academy, in contrast, is generally more sedate, and you can order food and wine from Andrew Edmunds, the excellent restaurant below.

To gain entry to these establishments you are supposed to be a member, but I would often get into Gerry's late at night by claiming to be a friend of the crime writer Martina Cole. All the booksellers on Charing Cross Road seemed to have honorary membership of the Phoenix. At the New Evaristo Club on Frith Street, aka Trisha's, aka Hideout, there's a sign saying 'Membership available' but I never met anyone who was a member. To me these places are only technically 'clubs' in order to circumvent normal licensing laws.

What they have in common is a dominant personality at the door or behind the bar. The Academy has Persian beauty Mandana Ruane and her team of small dogs. People tell me the Phoenix hasn't been the same since proprietor Maurice Huggett died in 2011. Dying too young is something of a theme of Soho clubs: Bernie Katz, the face of the Groucho, died in 2017. Michael Wojas went out aged 53 shortly after the Colony Room closed for good in 2008, and dear old Sebastian Horsley overdosed on heroin and cocaine in 2010. Being a legend of Soho takes its toll.

With London property prices the way they are, it's a miracle any drinking clubs still exist. They are an anachronism but, despite all the talk of London being a 24-hour city, they are often the only civilised places to get a drink after midnight. Treasure their dilapidated doorways, for they are portals into another world: the Soho of Keith Waterhouse or Julian MacLaren-Ross. Some mornings I'd emerge onto the streets of Soho, find my way home and sometime later think: did I dream that?

Notes on... Marmalade
Sophia Money-Coutts

Marmalade's had a rough old time of it lately. A report in the *Telegraph* declared it is dying out; that only oldies are buying it because millennials can't handle 'bits' in spreads. Well, excuse me, but I direct you to the World Marmalade Awards, held in a big Georgian house called Dalemain just outside Penrith, which attracted nearly 2,000 homemade jars from around the globe. Big jars, little jars, jars decorated with glitter, sticky jars that had leaked in the post, jars with gingham hats. All laid out on trestle tables with individual, handwritten tasting notes from the WI judges underneath, marking each jar out of 20.

The two-day festival has been running for nearly 20 years, launched by the matriarch of the house, Jane Hasell-McCosh, who grew up watching her grandmother make marmalade, standing on tiptoes to look into cauldrons of

the stuff on the Aga. With foot and mouth disease having devastated this patch of Cumbria in 2001, Jane decided to revive the area. 'It felt like the forgotten county, so I wanted to do something to help.' All proceeds go to local hospices.

She enlisted the support of the local WI to judge, along with Fortnum & Mason as a sponsor. In 2005, around 60 jars were sent in by enthusiastic locals. When I went in 2017, the number was not only in the thousands; it also attracted a record number of foreign entries from more than 30 countries. The Japanese ambassador was there too, invited as guest of honour. In a speech to launch the proceedings, His Excellency Koji Tsuruoka said he was glad to see so many jars 'made with love'. Marmalade is apparently 'huge' in Japan.

The jars were laid out in 14 categories (including 'Any Citrus', 'Dark and Chunky', 'Octogenarians and Upwards') across three wood-panelled rooms in the house. On one table – technically the 'International and Commonwealth Marmalade' category – was a jar of marmalade, lavender and mandarin from Belgium (13/20; 'good try' said its notes, slightly damningly), a jar of cardamom marmalade from the Czech Republic (17.5/20), and a whisky marmalade from Japan made from Banpeiyu citrus, a fruit originally from Malaysia. This was awarded 16/20; the spidery tasting notes observing that its peel 'wasn't quite cooked'.

Next door sat Eileen Wilson and Doreen Cameron, the two chief judges and members of the local WI, who have overseen the tasting of every jar sent in over the past three months. Dressed in their white lab coats, they watched hundreds of spectators and competitors mingle while they read out the judges' comments to one another. One woman who received 15/20 was dismayed to see she'd been marked down for letting 'too many pips' into her jar. Another, Johnny from Sussex, was ticked off for using old jars with previous labels attached. Marmalade hygiene is a serious business for Eileen and Doreen.

It rained, but that didn't matter: orangey bonhomie prevailed.

Notes on... Tapestries   Constance Watson

It is rare nowadays to see someone pull out a half-finished tapestry from their handbag and get on with their stitching. In fact, tapestry is becoming increasingly unfashionable; 'nomadic murals' (as architect Le Corbusier described them) are often relics of the distant past. So much so that they have plummeted in price.

'People are streaming into contemporary art, and tapestry is becoming more of a niche market,' says Marcus Radecke, Christie's European head of furniture. 'Whereas a large Brussels baroque tapestry might have fetched £50,000 in the 1980s or 1990s, nowadays it would sell for £20,000 or £25,000.'

That may still sound a lot for woven thread, but it's a long way short of the record-breaking $1.2 million paid for 'Wild Men', a Swiss medieval scene sold at Sotheby's in 1981. Another set called the Caesar tapestries was commissioned by Henry VIII. There were ten pieces, each 9 feet high and 25 feet long, and when hung in a row, they stretched 259 feet. The set was valued at £5,022 a century after the monarch's death, but sadly it disappeared at some point in the 19th century.

The price that tapestries could fetch were, and still can be, absurd. But see one up close and you will marvel at its glory. (The V&A has a fantastic collection, for starters, and I implore you to go and see them.)

Though domesticity is undergoing something of a renaissance – home-furnishing tycoons such as Cath Kidston have helped to make it fashionable again to think about what's on your walls and how fabrics look – tapestries seem to have been forgotten.

But they were to the medieval home what Kidston's Aga is to her kitchen. While aesthetically pleasing, their principal purpose was to keep the house warm. To the countryman, they were a vital addition to walls that were often damp.

At the National Trust's Hardwick Hall in Derbyshire, many of the rooms have tapestries in place of wallpaper, with paintings boldly hung over the scenes. The Devonshire Hunting Tapestries, on display in the V&A, were discovered at Hardwick, too.

There is something romantic about the congregational function that tapestries must have served: the thought of women gossiping and plotting over their canvases in times past is an exciting one. Bring back the stitch and bitch, I say.

Though it's not a discipline that will stave off Alzheimer's, as Sudoku claims to do, tapestry work can certainly be beneficial. Fine Cell Work is a brilliant social enterprise that trains prisoners to make everything from cushions to murals. It has recently teamed up with English Heritage to work on restoration projects. Their designs are modern and elegant, and show that tapestry has a place in the modern world.

Notes on... Boxer shorts Justin Marozzi

Chaps, be honest. Have you achieved nether-region nirvana? Twenty years ago I had reached the summit of underwear style and comfort but was haunted by the fear that one day I would come crashing down from these Elysian heights. My brand would go out of business and I would be confronting knicker nemesis. And sure enough, a while ago my fashionista friend Kitty Go duly reported that Regatta of Manila, purveyor of the world's most fabulous baggy boxers in the jauntiest fabrics, was no more. The crisis had struck.

Let's waste no time on jockeys, Y-fronts, briefs or those execrable jersey cotton hybrids or clingy lycra atrocities beloved by the clueless young. No, when a man is north of 40, he needs the tried and tested boxer short, named (so Shaun Cole's *The Story of Men's Underwear* tells me) after the heavyweight boxer Jack Dempsey, who won the 1919 world title in a pair of long loose shorts.

The best boxers provide support while allowing free movement and a spot of ventilation across the undercarriage. It's all in the gusset. My design guru friend Stephen Bayley, a boxers man too, says: 'Infrastructure is at least as important in building design as architecture. If the plumbing and underpinning don't work, no amount of surface finery will compensate. It's the same with getting dressed. The psychological advantages of wearing good socks and good underwear are truly profound. You will never achieve firmness and delight in plebeian Y-fronts or suffocating Lycra containers branded with the name of a has-been designer. When I step into my Brooks Brothers boxers I feel immediately dignified. I like my infrastructure to be Ivy League.'

I know what he means. I have tried popular brands like M&S, Boden, Gap and J. Crew but have always been left unsatisfied. Time to up the ante. Men's underwear is too frivolous not to take seriously.

I have road-tested some of the finest boxers in Britain. I have walked my dog in Norfolk's harshest mountain ranges, crossed deserts, sashayed through warzones and boulevardiered through the capital in a range of boxers to bring you this distillation of underwear wisdom.

My man in Budd, shirtmakers to the cognoscenti, kicks off with two models. One is nicknamed the Chairman's Briefs (£55), the other is known informally as the Buckingham Palace. 'They have the biggest ballroom in London.' I can attest to that. Both are fantastic. Derek Rose offers astonishingly luxurious silk boxers (£130), which had me begging for more. Their cotton counterparts (£35) are also excellent. Both score highly for having buttons on the waistband. A man likes to be undone from time to time.

Turnbull & Asser are shirtmakers to the King. Who knows whether they also provide him with boxers to house the crown jewels, but their Sea Island Cotton boxers (£70) offer royal levels of indulgence. Standard cotton is £50. These are among the roomiest here, with shades of Stanley Matthews bagginess circa 1953.

Honourable mentions go to the sumptuously Swiss underwear maestros Zimmerli (€54), Jermyn Street shirtmaker Harvie and Hudson (£30), Hamilton and Hare, who offer a thrilling, very athletic take on the boxer (£32), Burtonwode (£24) and Beaufort & Blake (£20). Boxer bliss achieved.

Notes on... The Surrey Hills Christopher Winn

I live in the oldest village in England. How come? Well, in a field below the big house, there is a Mesolithic pit dwelling dating back some 10,000 years. This is the oldest known man-made dwelling in England – at least according to Dr Louis Leakey, who excavated it and wrote about it in *The Spectator* in December 1950. Prehistoric man instinctively knew that the Surrey Hills are a wonderful place in which to live.

Today, I suspect most people see them as a slightly blurry backdrop to the annual RideLondon-Surrey cycle infestation. I see them as a paradise.

Surrey is England's most wooded county and if you drive east from Guildford, birthplace of P.G. Wodehouse and possessed of 'the most beautiful high street in England', according to Charles Dickens, you enter a magical land of hills and trees, carpeted blue in spring, dappled green in summer, blazing red and gold in autumn.

On the banks of the mysterious Silent Pool, where Agatha Christie parked her car and disappeared in 1926, is Albury, England's smallest vineyard. (The Silent Pool Rosé produced here was served aboard the royal barge during the Diamond Jubilee river pageant.) Next to Albury Park, where George III's coronation banquet was held in 1761, a beautiful Saxon church hides a secret chapel, richly decorated in dazzling colours by Pugin for banker Henry Drummond. The rector here in the 17th century was William Oughtred, inventor of the slide rule and the multiplication sign (x) and tutor to Christopher Wren. Oughtred, who 'died of ecstasy' at the Restoration of Charles II, lies somewhere among the Saxon stones.

The gardens at Albury were laid out – with what was once the longest yew hedge in the world – by the diarist John Evelyn, who also created England's first Italian garden at Wotton House, his ancestral home a few miles away. Evelyn, whose grandfather introduced gunpowder to England, was a noted herbalist and gives his name in part to those purveyors of fine soaps and fragrances Crabtree & Evelyn.

The grounds of Wotton House occupy the slopes of Leith Hill, the highest point in southeast England, made a mountain by the tower at its summit, from which there are glorious views – north to London, south across the Weald to the South Downs and the sea. Below is Leith Hill Place, now part of the National Trust and where, on the occasional enchanted summer evening, you can hear a performance of 'The Lark Ascending' in the very garden where Ralph Vaughan Williams grew up and first heard a lark, er, ascending. To the east, on Pitch Hill, is the garden where George Harrison wrote 'Here Comes the Sun'. There's music in these here hills.

And so to Dorking, where Nelson spent his last night in England, birthplace of Laurence Olivier and home to England's biggest vineyard, Denbies, as well as the only surviving house of a Mayflower pilgrim father, William Mullins, a shoemaker whose descendants include four presidents and Marilyn Monroe. I rest my case.

Notes on... The Cathars James Delingpole

I once spent three months living in the Languedoc, writing my first novel. The highlight was the few days I allowed myself away from my monastic schedule to visit Cathar country. I'd been dying to see it because the castles and the landscape are so stark and dramatic, the history is so dark, bloody and weird, and because I wanted to try cassoulet in its proper location.

I can't remember much about the various cassoulets I tried except that, though it's impossible to go wrong with goose, sausage and beans, none of them was quite as good as the one I laboriously recreated at home from a recipe in my *Larousse Gastronomique*. But you never forget the castles, such as Peyrepertuse, jutting, as so many of them do, from a vertiginous, craggy, razor-back ridge. I clambered over it at dusk, after it had closed, and had it all to myself. The wind whistled (it was December) and it was so easy to imagine the ghosts of those who had lived and died there, many of them horribly.

The Cathars were a heretical sect who believed (probably correctly) that their Gnostic version of Christianity – simple, honest, virtuous – was truest to the original. Naturally, the Catholic Church hated them for this and tried to eradicate them in numerous purges, culminating in the Albigensian Crusade launched by Pope Innocent III. It was prosecuted with a savagery redolent of Isis's persecution of the Yazidis in northern Iraq. When the crusaders reached Béziers, the Papal legate sent out a message to its Catholic citizens that they should hand over the leading Cathars and spare themselves. The citizens refused and every last one – as many as 20,000 – was slaughtered. Many burned alive in the cathedral. 'Kill them all and let God sort them out,' the legate infamously commanded.

Once it was all over and the last Cathars had been hanged, burned at the stake or driven into the wilds, the Catholic Church celebrated by building probably the world's most magnificently ugly cathedral in Albi, thought to be the heresy's centre. Wide and vast, with a turret-like belltower at one end, built from red brick, it wasn't designed with beauty in mind: it was meant to be like a fortress, signalling to the local populace the total, crushing domination of the church. It's horrible but I kind of love it – and the interior is much prettier than the exterior.

Finally Carcassonne, which inspired the world's most addictive tile-centric strategy game (seriously: just get it!), and which is probably the closest you'll ever get to experiencing the perfect fantasy medieval castle, with drawbridges, a moat, and turrets with conical roofs. You can imagine Rapunzel letting down her hair here – or Shrek climbing to meet Princess Fiona.

It's all a sham, of course. Which is to say, it was heavily restored in the mid-19th century by the architect Eugène Viollet-le-Duc. But it's still gorgeously romantic, though best visited outside the main tourist season – I went at Christmas, when the weather was so warm you rarely needed more than a T-shirt – because being a Unesco world heritage site, it does get awfully crowded. Book a table in one of the many good restaurants within its walls. Lunch is the perfect time for cassoulet: you need time to walk off all that unctuous grease, stodge and deliciousness.

Notes on... Wetherspoons Henry Jefferys

Of all the stories I've heard about the fallout from Brexit – families divided, work jeopardised, friendships ended – the saddest was someone on Facebook who declared that he would never again visit a Wetherspoons because the proprietor, Tim Martin, pushed for a Leave vote. This seemed to me the definition of cutting your nose off to spite your face; imagine turning down cheap beer because of the EU! But it also disrupts one of the fundamentals of a liberal society: that you do business even with those whom you disagree. Voltaire marvelled at this concept on his visit to the London Stock Exchange: 'Here Jew, Mohammedan and Christian deal with each other as though they were all of the same faith, and only apply the word infidel to people who go bankrupt.'

But it's then long been fashionable to sneer at Wetherspoons. Perhaps it's because they sell such cheap beer. In London a pint in Wetherspoons will cost you less than two thirds of what you'll pay in the place with gastro pretensions up the hill. They can offer these prices because they have massive buying power: more than 1,000 pubs around the country. It's a far cry from when Tim Martin bought his first pub in 1979 and decided to name the company after one of

his old teachers who couldn't control the class – which was how Martin felt about trying to run a pub.

It has to be said, those prices do mean that you get some colourful characters in a Spoons. The one in Liverpool Street station is particularly intimidating, full of loud men with shaven heads having a few before their trains back to Billericay. In a cavernous converted bank or cinema – typical Spoons venues – you're not going to get the burble of conversation, the crackle of an open fire and the landlord's wife's shepherd's pie.

So by the standards of that mythical pub we all have in our minds, Wetherspoons falls short. But then so do 99 per cent of pubs. Most are owned by chains. One of the biggest, Mitchells & Butlers, also own Nicholson's, Harvester and All Bar One. Many pubs that look independent aren't: our local in Blackheath, the Hare & Billet, is owned by the Metropolitan Pub Company. But being part of a chain doesn't stop your average Wetherspoons from being something of a drinker's paradise. Whereas until recently many pubs considered doing real ale a chore, Wetherspoons have always prided themselves on their selection. The food isn't bad either (I recommend the curries and the meat pies). In a strange town, a Spoons can be a refuge.

As with all chains, there are good Spoons and bad. The best have a sense of community lacking in more upmarket neighbours where the regulars have been priced out. I experienced the full magic recently at the Brockley Barge in south-east London. The beer, of course, was good and cheap – but even better was the atmosphere. There were postmen enjoying a post-work drink, students, old men eking out their pensions and chubby girls drinking pinot grigio by the bucketload. People were smiling and talking to each other. Maybe I'd had too much discount real ale, but that night I felt like Voltaire at the London Stock Exchange. However you voted in the referendum, can we at least agree that being able to buy a pint of Timothy Taylor's Landlord for under £5 is a wonderful thing?

Notes on... Doorsteps James Innes-Smith

Every general election, you hear a lot about doorsteps. Politicians love to demonstrate how much they care about ordinary, hard-working voters by banging on about how many front doors they've knocked on. Standing on a doorstep, preferably in the driving rain, proves how dedicated you are to getting your message of 'hope' and 'change' across.

An hour or two trekking through provincial avenues, camera crew in tow, pays dividends back at the TV studio where you can then boast about how many of the electorate are on your side. Of course the reality of doorstepping is much bleaker. Politicians rarely tell you about the utter dreariness of hanging around on other people's shabby stoops; the miserable old gits yelling at you to bugger off back to 'that London'; the furious 'just-about-managing's shooing you away with complaints about the rubbish not being taken away often enough. You never hear politicians bragging about how many doors were slammed in their faces or about the avalanches of abuse.

Doorstep trawling mostly involves travelling 'up and down' the country. Sometimes it's the 'length and breadth'; but mostly it's up and down, the M1 making it possible to be in and out of a marginal Midlands seat in no time. Pounding doorsteps shows how willing you are to listen to voters' concerns. In reality, of course, it's about telling them what they want to hear; that and boasting about how well the economy is doing or how much better it would be doing if only they would swap sides.

Politicians are choosy about the kind of doorsteps they visit. They seem particularly enamoured of those boringly respectable 1930s types, the ones with little glass porches and doorbells; the sort lived in by 'hard-working families'. You rarely see an honourable member knocking on the handsomely lintelled door of another, very different kind of honourable's grand Elizabethan pile. And you hardly ever spot inner-city politicians loitering outside those trendy warehouse developments in Shoreditch. That's because the bearded hipster and the castled viscount are unlikely to be swayed by an impromptu visit and a gaudy, patronising leaflet. Besides, politicians aren't supposed to care what aristos and hipsters think. As a result, the more attractively rendered doorsteps tend to be ignored – although I would pay good money to watch Keir Starmer being rained on outside Blenheim Palace's immaculately sculpted Vanbrugh porch, soggy leaflet in hand.

The rule of thumb seems to be that if you are going to continue badgering voters in the privacy of their own homes, make sure the doorsteps you choose have seen better days but are not too knackered; the ones that could do with a bit of a makeover and a new welcome mat but have not been over-gentrified. Oh, and make sure the doors have functioning letterboxes for when the owners are out – or pretending to be.

Notes on... Ruislip Lido William Cook

Most mornings, if I'm not too hungover, I go for a run around Ruislip Lido – a mile there, through Ruislip Woods, about two miles round the lido and a mile back again. It generally takes me about half an hour. On my way, I see woodpeckers, egrets, sparrowhawks, and the occasional Muntjac deer. It's hard to believe you're in London, at the arse end of the Metropolitan line, surrounded by bland suburbia – John Betjeman's Metroland.

Ruislip Woods is the largest slice of natural woodland in Greater London: 726 acres of oak, beech and hornbeam, and the lido is its pearl. People have gathered timber from this scruffy forest since god knows when. The medieval barn at Ruislip Manor is built from oaks that were saplings here 1,000 years ago, when these wild woods stretched right across Middlesex, Bucks and Herts.

Naturally, Ruislip Lido isn't quite so ancient. It was built 200 years ago as a reservoir for the Grand Union Canal, but the idea was a failure. The canal was too far away and the reservoir flooded local farms. For more than a century it lay forgotten, a gigantic puddle on the edge of London, until the canal company had the bright idea of turning it into a lido. They built a splendid Art Deco pavilion, dumped some sand along the shore, and opened up the reservoir for bathing and boating. Trains and charabancs brought day trippers from the Big Smoke – a cheap day out for Londoners at an ersatz seaside resort.

Its glory days were after the war, before cheap package holidays. They built a miniature railway and held beauty contests, and happy families and courting couples flooded in. Jon Pertwee went waterskiing, Cliff Richard filmed *The Young Ones*, and 19-year-old Charlotte Rampling reclined on a speedboat in her swimsuit to drum up publicity for a movie called *The Knack*.

But in the 1970s and 1980s the punters started disappearing to Spain and the Ruislip Riviera lost its lustre. The pavilion burned down. The turnstiles rusted over. Bathing was prohibited. The pedalos were packed away. When I moved to Ruislip five years ago the lido seemed rather run down, a sad relic of a bygone era, and the surrounding woods felt seedy. I have no evidence to support this theory – it's probably the product of a dirty mind – but some secluded areas had that distinctive 'dogging' vibe. The foliage was festooned with beer cans and vodka bottles. I didn't want to look too closely at what else might be lying around.

Yet lately something's changed. The council has built a smart new 'Woodland Centre' and spruced up the public areas. There's a children's playground, an outdoor gym, and the miniature railway is still there. The lido has been recolonised by joggers, dog walkers, and all sorts of nesting birds. When my daughter went there on a school trip, I tagged along. She spent an idyllic afternoon fishing for tiddlers. We walked home through the woods together and it was one of the best days out I've had in years.

You're still not allowed to swim in it (something to do with pollution, apparently) and sailing remains verboten (the water level is too low), but I rather like the absurdist concept of a lido you can't take a dip in. It's a perfect fit for Ruislip, this surreal suburb where medieval England and Betjeman's Metroland collide.

Notes on... Pub quizzes
Marcus Berkmann

For more than 20 years now, I have been trudging up the hill to the Prince of Wales in Highgate on Tuesday evenings to take part in that tiny pub's venerable weekly quiz. Each evening promises something different and yet somehow the same: ferocious competition, ridiculous arguments over the answer to question four, several glasses of red wine and usually, during round three, a few packets of Sweet Thai Chilli Sensations crisps. The quiz is unusual in that it is set by its regulars, and I have hosted 178. That's more than 8,000 questions, allowing for the odd repeat.

Why do we do it? In 1993, pub quizzing was an occupation of the severest eccentricity, but like Donald Trump it has gradually been normalised. Pub owners are particularly keen, because quiz teams drink an awful lot. Whether this is because they are infected by natural high spirits or because they are a load of drunks is often the subject of fevered debate. This is in contrast to people who go to the pub to watch football,

who habitually drink as little as they can get away with.

We do it, we have decided, for two related reasons. One is that it is a form of play for grown-ups who don't get to play much in their lives. Whatever else is going on, we can forget about all that for two blissful hours while we try and name all five English kings (since 1066) who succeeded their brothers. The second reason is showing off. Most of us are middle-aged and few of us will now represent our country in any sort of high-level sport – but if we can remember that the only airline with three successive letters as its name is KLM, we can punch the air and cheer noisily as though at Wembley or Lord's. It's these adrenaline rushes, and the realisation that all that education you once endured was for something after all, that brings you back for more, week after week.

The pub quiz has changed, there's no doubt about that. The questions have become tougher and, in our pub at least, more baroque. Music rounds, a staple a decade ago, have been all but abandoned because of the wide disparity in listening tastes between older and younger teams. (Older teams have never knowingly heard Justin Bieber. Younger teams seem to have heard little else.) But I'm glad to say that our humble quiz continues to attract a better class of contestant. There was a *Mastermind* winner in the other day, and one of the Chasers from *The Chase* is a regular. Our team used to win much of the time, but our best player made the terrible mistake of dying, so we are generally fifth and grumbling these days. The grumbling is good fun too, of course.

And the five English kings who succeeded their brothers? Henry I, John, James II, William IV and George VI. Five points if you got all of them. (We forgot Henry I, needless to say.)

Notes on... Corduroy Marcus Berkmann

Every Christmas, I ask my loved ones for at least two pairs of corduroy trousers. Off with a sigh tramps my girlfriend, who knows that fashion cycles dictate that corduroy will be 'in', and therefore purchasable, only every fourth or fifth year or so. For three or four years corduroy will be invisible. Shop assistants will look askance at anyone who dares even mention it. Then corduroy is rediscovered by whoever decides these things, and it's everywhere. Cushions are in corduroy. Dogs wear corduroy. I saw a corduroy tie the other day. At such times we corduroy lovers stock up, conscious of the long corduroy-free winter that will inevitably follow.

I bought my first two pairs of corduroy trousers in 1979, when I was at university. One was blue, one was brown, they were both thick corduroy and I wore them both with great pleasure. Until one day I happened to be present when two of my friends decided to ingest some magic mushrooms. One of them is now dead (nothing to do with mushrooms), the other is an eminent and extremely rich merchant banker. Like many drug neophytes, they wondered why the mushrooms weren't working and so took some more – far too many, as it turns out. I was there in an observational capacity (i.e. to take them to hospital if it all went wrong) and they decided, among other things, that my brown corduroy trousers were watching them. Indeed, after the drugs had worn off, these remained 'the watching trousers', and both of my friends reacted with alarm, leaching into abject terror, whenever they saw me wearing them. So obviously I did wear them, possibly a little too often.

Did I become a writer because of my fondness for corduroy? Or did my writerly leanings propel me in a corduroy direction? I'm not sure I care, to be honest, but I would say that there remains a fellowship of corduroy-wearers that transcends all other considerations. If you see a fellow scribbler wearing a natty corduroy suit, it is perfectly acceptable for you to fawn all over him and ask where he got it, because corduroy suits are rarer than beluga caviar and rather more expensive. He won't tell you, of course, because he has found a supply and he means to keep it for himself. The fellowship only goes so far.

There are downsides, of course. Corduroy is the only known multi-media fabric, in that you can usually hear it coming. Wiff-wiff-wiff go the brushing legs of corduroy trousers, or WIFF-WIFF-WIFF if they're flared. Although theoretically hard-wearing, it has a tendency to go bald and threadbare surprisingly quickly. If you are not careful you can go from debonair man about town to tramp in a matter of weeks. I had a green corduroy suit I particularly liked, and the trousers became so compromised you could see daylight through them. The jacket remains in perfect nick, and sits in the cupboard, tragically unworn.

But I love a corduroy suit because it's a way of wearing a suit without really wearing a suit, if you see what I mean. You have all the conveniences without the dreary connotations. Either that or you're a geography teacher. It's definitely one of the two.

Notes on... Hangovers Katy Balls

Although drinking excessive levels of alcohol is up there with Olympic cycling and democracy as things the British excel at, the same cannot be said for dealing with the aftermath. Over the festive season we splash more than £2 billion on trips to the pub as punters take exhortations to have a merry Christmas a bit too literally. But our subsequent hangovers cost the economy almost £260 million through sick days and a lack of productivity.

A night on the tiles tends to leave people feeling a little defenceless the next day. However, for those of us who have no option but to be bright-eyed and bushy-tailed in the morning, there are measures that can be taken to limit the pain. As a former newspaper diarist, I've learned what to avoid when presented with trays of booze.

As with most sickness, prevention is better than cure. While not drinking boasts a 100 per cent success rate, this is not always a satisfactory option. So careful drink selection is the next best method. As a general rule, avoid martinis full stop. Dukes – the bar that inspired Bond's catchphrase 'shaken not stirred' – have got it right with their no-more-than-two rule. 007 may ignore it, but you should not.

The next thing to look out for is colour. The darker the drink, the worse the hangover. This is thanks to congeners, the chemicals that give drinks their distinctive flavour and are most abundant in spirits like whiskey and cognac.

By contrast, translucent drinks contain hardly any. Of these, champagne is the best, as its fast alcohol absorption rate means it is unlikely to hit you when it's all too late.

For those with tighter purse strings, there's its more modest cousin, wine. While the hangover will be less catastrophic than after a night on the bourbon, the night itself could be equally traumatic, if not more so. The term 'white wine rage' has a place in popular culture thanks to the emotional wreck one can become after 250ml of chardonnay. Rumour has it that it's the sulphites – which have been linked to depression – though others suggest it's the fact that a bottle tends to follow the first glass.

As for red, this presents double danger, because even if you do get away hangover-free, your 'red wine lips' will tell a different story the next day at work.

If you still wake up bleary-eyed, feeling queasy and low, there are a few options left on the table. Should drinking your weight in full-fat Coke not appeal, hair of the dog can do the trick, but you will just be putting off the inevitable. So, it can be best to push through and opt for mind over matter. Or in the words of Kingsley Amis – an authoritative voice on the subject: 'You are not sickening for anything, you have not suffered a minor brain lesion, you are not all that bad at your job, your family and friends are not leagued in a conspiracy of barely maintained silence about what a shit you are, you have not come at last to see life as it really is and there is no use crying over spilt milk.'

Notes on... A good night's sleep
Laura Freeman

Have you, on hearing the story of the princess who felt a pea through 40 feather mattresses, ever thought that she was, well, a bit of a wet blanket? One measly dried pea through all that padding and she wakes up black and blue with bruises? 'I can't tell you what I've suffered!' she quivers in an 1846 English translation from the Hans Christian Andersen original.

Ah, but you don't know the whole story. Go back to Andersen and you discover it

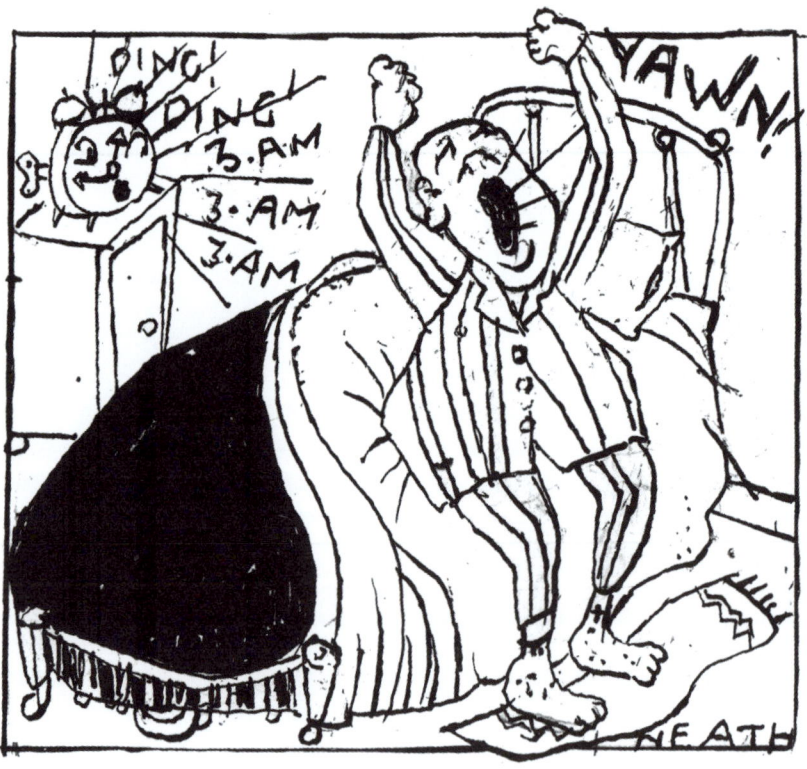

was *three* peas. Poor princess. Now I understand. Imagine fidgeting in the night, feeling a lump under the mattress, and rolling over to the cool side of the bed and finding another pea – dastardly pea – and curling up miserably at the foot of the bed only to discover a third pea-hummock. Imagine looking down from the height of 40 mattresses and finding that the Queen has taken the ladder away so you can't even try one of the palace's 27 spare rooms, or the billiard table, or a soft-looking bit of marble floor. No wonder she didn't sleep.

I am in sympathy with the princess because I, too, am a bad sleeper. I, too, wake from two hours' rest on the coir matting in the sitting room, warp and weft printed into my cheek, and tremble across the breakfast table: 'Black and blue. Can't tell you what I've suffered.'

I toss, I turn, I throw off the quilt, kick out the hot-water bottle, turn the pillows, wriggle bed socks off or on, fluff the duvet, count sheep, count my breaths, count to 100, 1,000, 10,000. I make hot milk, dab temples with lavender. I try the sofa, I try the floor. I listen to a Nigel Slater audio book. 'Tunnock's Teacake… Sunday roast… Blackpool rock.'

Somewhere between 'Dairylea Triangles' and 'Farmers' markets' I fall asleep. At five I am awake, exhausted, and without even a prince's hand in marriage to show for it.

By day, I press my nose to the windows of mattress shops as other women do displays of chocolates or handbags. They have such lovely names; names that promise so much: And So To Bed, Dreams, Silentnight, Savoir. Doesn't that last sound like someone just dropping-off and starting to snore? Savoirrrrr…

Would a new mattress, new linen, new goose-feather pillows make the difference? In the shops I stroke 500-thread-count sheets and squeeze eiderdown duvets and lie down in my coat on £3,000 mattresses. Would these turn me from ugly insomniac duckling into immaculate Sleeping Beauty swan?

One other detail from the Andersen story. After the princess has proved herself – 'for it was quite impossible for any one but a true princess to be so tender' – she is married to the prince and the three peas are deposited in the national museum.

You can still see them now, says Andersen, if they have not been lost. The princess, blast her, peas safely behind glass, sleeps happily ever after.

Notes on... Coming second Mark Mason

Who was the second prime minister? Everyone knows Robert Walpole was the first. Firsts get all the fame and glory. But what about the poor seconds, elbowed into the shadows of history? Isn't it time they were given some love? Step forward, the Earl of Wilmington, PM from 1742 to 1743. Let us celebrate the fact that his country house in Warwickshire appeared as a monastery in *Carry On Camping* – and was the inspiration for Croft Manor, Lara's childhood home in the *Tomb Raider* games.

Likewise, no one knows very much about James Garfield, the second US president to be assassinated. I certainly didn't until I researched him for my new book, *The Book of Seconds*. I didn't know that he could write in Latin with one hand and, simultaneously, in Greek with the other. I didn't know that he took weeks to die: a bullet remained lodged in his body, and Alexander Graham Bell invented a metal detector to find it. He failed, but only because the doctors incorrectly thought the bullet was on Garfield's right side and wouldn't let Bell use it on the left.

The ultimate second is Apollo 12. Once Neil and Buzz had done their thing, no one cared about Pete Conrad and Alan Bean. But the pair were far more interesting than their predecessors. On the way to the moon they danced weightlessly to 'Sugar Sugar' by the Archies. Alan Bean left his silver Nasa badge on the lunar surface, knowing his mission had earned him a gold one. Pete Conrad ended up doing an American Express advert based on the fact that no one recognised him. It made him more famous than he'd become by walking on the moon.

Some seconds seem particularly unfair. Peter Norman won silver in the 200 metres at the 1968 Mexico Olympics – but all anyone remembers is Tommie Smith (gold) and John Carlos (bronze) giving the black power salute on the podium. Yet it was Norman who, when Carlos forgot his gloves, suggested they each wear one of Smith's pair. That's why in the famous picture Smith is lifting his right arm and Carlos his left.

Other seconds, however, seem content with their anonymity. AC/DC's Brian Johnson speaks of the band deliberately staying 'below the radar', and always wears his cap pulled well down. That's why you probably don't know that *Back in Black* is the second best-selling album ever (behind *Thriller*). The bell that opens the LP was made to order. The band had tried recording the one in Loughborough's war memorial tower, but whenever it sounded pigeons flew off and ruined the take.

Second-largest island, after Greenland? That would be New Guinea, whose main language is Tok Pisin, known as New Guinea Pidgin. It has some wonderful expressions. 'Hair' is gras bilong het ('head grass'), while a helicopter is magimiks bilong Yesus, or 'Jesus's Magimix'. When the then Prince Charles visited in 2012 he introduced himself as *nambawan pikinini bilong misis kwin* – 'number one child of Mrs Queen'.

So seconds can hold all sorts of wonder. Saturn, for example, might not be as big as Jupiter. But it's the only planet that's less dense than water. Which means that, were you able to find a bath big enough, Saturn would float in it.

Notes on... Kites Christopher Fletcher

I've flown only three kites in my life. My stepfather bought me the first. I remember seeing him from a window approaching our little mews house off Bond Street, clutching it furled in its packet as though his life depended upon it.

The previous day he had overcharged an electric plane sent for my birthday by my other father, the one left in America following a youthful marriage that didn't pan out. The walk to the launch took us past the barley-twist facades of Mount Street and Allens the butchers (alas, no more) whose soft light, sawdust and warm meaty air I always recall pooling the pavement on autumn trudges home from St George's primary school. From the centre of Hyde Park the plane hopped jauntily onto the breeze and kept going until it crossed Park Lane, rose above the hotels and swanky showrooms, resolved into an agitated dot, and disappeared.

The kite, however, had strings attached and would not fly away. Shortly after that, Peter became Dad.

The second was made by my grandfather. A taciturn Scot, his affection burst out in occasional acts of madness that punctuate thrillingly the memories of my 1970s childhood. '100… 105… 108… 111!' he once counted through clenched teeth, hands gripped on the wheel of his mustard Rover V8 as I pressed my nose to the windscreen, the lane lines of the M20 coming at me like tracer fire. Once, barrelling through the Dartford Tunnel late at night, a Tannoy boomed at him to 'Slow down!' For a moment he thought it was God.

The kite was formidable, a garage-special lash-up of polythene, wrist-thick dowl and industrial insulating tape. When he let my sister and me take charge, we scudded along the ground like cloud shadows made flesh.

The third was this summer, bought from a seaside shop on Sandyhills Bay on the southern coast of Galloway; a cheap confection of coloured plastic and weedy string. It was my daughter's first. As darkening clouds grumbled at us from the hills, she dug into her mind's flickering traces of kids' telly to tell me about Benjamin Franklin sending up his key in a storm. Who cares? Up, up and away it went, such a flimsy thing now bodied out and tense.

Sandyhills is a sweet, tidy resort on a vast tidal stretch. The water comes in so fast that someone once apparently raced the sea to shore on a thoroughbred, just making it. Walking out a few hundred yards with my daughter made me feel uncanny; the feeling I had, in fact, when my stepdad, in his suede belted jacket, fruitlessly ran after the one-trick plane, leaving me quite alone in the dizzying green space of the park. Perfect for flying, though, and my daughter was rapt, tugging and squinting up at the thing angrily anchoring her to the sky.

Her own nature is moving on. Half the time was spent flying the kite, throwing balls for our Shetland sheepdog, digging holes and making and smashing sandcastles. The other was seeking out spangly crop tops in the M&Co in Castle Douglas; gobbling up mobile data to keep pace with unmentionable reality shows; and sketching out girlie outfits with yet another set of coloured pens.

Why, oh why, did I wait until she was ten, and I past 50, to go kite-flying again?

Notes on... Unst Ted Harrison

'I'd like a copy of the *Times*,' said the visitor from the south. 'Yesterday's or today's?' the shopkeeper asked. 'Today's, of course.' 'Come back tomorrow.'

Life on Unst (population: 600) has its idiosyncrasies, but personally, I blame the weather forecasters for giving the nation the impression that the place may not even exist. Their London-centric maps of Britain, showing Scotland fading into the distance, leave us off entirely. Not surprising, as we are the most northern of the Shetland Islands and nearer Bergen than Aberdeen. Newcastle is to us the deep south.

Yet we hold a key position in defence. It wasn't a coincidence that when Kim Jong-un started building rockets, it was announced that the RAF base on the island would be taken out of mothballs. Should the North Koreans lob a missile over the pole, Unst is the first British land it would reach.

On the subject of rockets, there's talk of Unst becoming the UK's Cape Canaveral. The island, we were told at a recent community consultation, is ideally placed for launching satellites into polar orbit. The satellites would be scarcely bigger than biscuit tins and the small rockets needed for launch, we were reassured, wouldn't incinerate the wildlife.

We enjoy a busy tourist season. Visitors arrive by caravan-ette, or bicycle, via three ferries from the British mainland. Alternatively they fly into the airport on Shetland mainland and hire cars. They come with binoculars and backpacks, anoraks and anticipation – excited to reach the most northerly tip of the United Kingdom and take selfies with the Muckle Flugga lighthouse as a backdrop.

Then they visit the most northerly gin distillery, most northerly tearoom, shop, castle, church and post office (to have their postcards franked with a puffin postmark) before heading south again. Not forgetting of course to sign the visitors' book at the bus shelter, which has its own internet presence, and is newly decorated every year. In 2018 the theme was the centenary of women's suffrage. Alongside there's a large model of a puffin, wearing an Emmeline Pankhurst sash.

It is one of a dozen such puffins around the island used for the annual UnstFest puffin hunt. UnstFest is, unsurprisingly, Britain's most northerly festival. The programme once included the creation of the world's longest golf course: nine holes stretching the ten-mile length of the island.

Nature lovers are guaranteed sightings of seals, while the lucky ones will spot an otter or two. The very lucky might see the Shetland killer whales. Many of the breeding birds have migrated south, but September is twitcher season. When some disorientated, rare foreign bird lands on Unst, the keenest birders have been known to charter planes to get here as fast as they can.

The short days and long nights of winter are when the community comes into its own. There are two fire festivals when squads of Vikings carry burning torches to the seashore. Everything will be battened down as the gales are sure to blow: the strongest wind ever recorded in Britain was here. And on still and clear frosty nights you might see the merry dancers, the Northern Lights, flash across the sky. We call Unst the island above all others – and we mean it.

Notes on... Being the perfect guest Lucy Deedes

Come to our house in France, say generous friends, come to Italy, come fishing. 'How wonderful, what shall we bring?' Nothing, they reply. They are lying, obviously. Bring cash, a thoughtful present for the house – pillowcases, new books – and your biggest smile. You don't want the hosts rolling their eyes and punching the air when you drive away down that olive grove.

The thing is, it's not a hotel. There are people who can be a little peremptory with their friends' staff. There is no point during the day or night when the dishwasher won't need emptying and the cook will be delighted if you do that – extra points for cleaning the filter – or lay the table, wash the lettuce or do the bread run before breakfast.

Try to dissuade the children from water bombs and shouty swimming during that post-lunch snoozy hush around the pool. We'll enjoy little Angelica's diving later. Perhaps a nice book in the shade for an hour? (No, mine neither.)

Offer to take the household out to dinner. Everything you eat and drink has been thought through, written on lists, bought, carted home, cooked and served for your delight. They've earned an evening off.

If there's more than one of you, hire a car so you can be independent, which your hosts will like. Then at least you're not always standing around on the terrace with your hat on, bothering someone to drive you to the market/chemist/village.

We all have our little food habits and breakfast can be fraught with drama. No holiday breakfast would be complete without someone opening the fridge door and shrieking. If a child has drunk your almond milk or fed your chia seeds to the birds, keep calm and have a lovely warm white roll with apricot jam like everyone else. You're on holiday! Things are different there.

Many of us have a pet subject upon which, given a starting pistol and a patient listener, we can drone on a bit. It may be golf, your garden, your children or perhaps you just always know best. Unlike one's children, who will not hesitate to say: 'You've told me that before,' your fellow guests may be too polite. If people start slipping sideways off their chairs, it's a clue.

Try not to tell your host how to drive his boat, even if you are a big dog in the Royal Yacht Squadron. And no bitching around the pool: sound carries nicely over water.

Get the tipping right and if in doubt, ask your host. Happy staff means happy holidays.

Relax. Read a book, paint, play a game. There's nothing more tiring than someone jingling car keys and asking what today's plan is. Your hosts have admin to do such as spraying the bugs on the box hedges; they love a guest who can amuse himself, and others. Agree to all plans and last-minute changes with equanimity and they'll feel it was worth it.

And teenagers: feel free to try any of this at home.

Notes on... Frankincense and myrrh
David Abulafia

'And when they were come into the house, they saw the young child with Mary his mother, and fell down, and worshipped him: and when they had opened their treasures, they presented unto him gifts: gold, and frankincense, and myrrh.' About 15 years ago, a colleague at Cambridge was returning from a visit to Yemen. The British customs officers asked him what he had bought, and he declared that his luggage contained frankincense and myrrh. 'And gold as well, I suppose!' came the ironic reply, and he was let through without further ado. Later, he gave me a brown paper bag filled with nuggets of myrrh, which I used to hand round at my lectures when talking about the history of the trade in perfumes and spices, inviting my audience to chew a piece.

It may have done them some good. The label of an upmarket toothpaste will often reveal that it contains myrrh. Its medical benefits are said to extend to leprosy (suiting its biblical background) and it may kill off all sorts of bacteria and viruses, though whether it was used in Trump's White House during Covid has not been revealed.

But it has always been used mainly for its smell. Myrrh retains its perfume longer than any other aromatic. Both frankincense and myrrh are gum resins that contain volatile oils. Some 3,000 years ago their cultivation spread over large tracts of Eritrea and South Arabia, which were wetter and more fertile than nowadays. One can wait for the trees to exude a sticky liquid, and collect that; or (if in a hurry) one can make incisions in the bark out of which oil will seep.

Frankincense and myrrh were the prestige products of the earliest trade routes to navigate down the Red Sea. The Pharaohs burned masses of myrrh before the Egyptian gods when they returned in triumph from war. Plenty of myrrh was used for embalming the dead, which might explain the acute interest of the female Pharaoh Hatshepsut in sending a fleet of magnificent ships to acquire it along with lions, giraffes, ivory and other exotica a few years before she died in 1458 BC.

In the time of Jesus, the incense used in the Jewish Temple was very carefully mixed from a great variety of ingredients, beaten fine: 11 spices, including frankincense, myrrh, saffron, cinnamon and Cyprus wine. This was the time when Petra flourished, thanks to the Nabataean myrrh traders. South Arabian incense travelled overland via Petra in their camel caravans. During the Middle Ages, massive cargoes of frankincense and myrrh were loaded on ships and taken all the way across the Indian Ocean and the South China Sea to the imperial court in China.

Modern myrrh may not be appreciated quite so much in Heaven. I bought a packet of incense cones made out of the two resins in York this summer – 15 cones for £1. The packet promises me 'spiritual

enlightenment' when I burn a cone, which I am doing as I write. Has that ever worked? An ancient Israelite altar, recently discovered in the Negev Desert, shows that its priests burned frankincense on one altar and cannabis on another. Maybe that altar kept them happy, but I don't think frankincense or myrrh induced any trances.

Notes on... Literary motorcycling
Christopher Fletcher

No seat belts. No airbags. Just air, and coming at you as fast as you like. Motorcycling shouldn't be allowed, really, but thank God it is. Hanging on to an engine braced between two wheels as you travel through the countryside is worth any dose of mindfulness. The NHS should prescribe it. Even with the cost of broken bones and, alas, the occasional overheads of the mortuary, it would save money on mental health treatments.

Your senses are stimulated in a way that is impossible in a car, with the force of movement intensifying an ordinary experience. Smells and temperature become suddenly distinct as you dip or rise, fly through conifer or broad leaf, past farmyards and bonfires. Other traffic on a good sweeping road becomes an irrelevance. You just fire past it as your arms stretch and eyes weep in the welt of acceleration.

I have taken to riding regularly with an old friend of my wife about whom I never worried much until I discovered he was a regular petrolhead. Our trips have, through accident, become small literary pilgrimages. First we ended up in Stratford. A short leather-creaking distance from the centre, we paid tribute to Shakespeare in Holy Trinity Church. Apparently he and four of his family lie only three feet below the surface, unencased and in shrouds.

On our next trip, heading back from the Ace Café, 1950s hangout of the Ton-up Boys, we dropped into Stoke Poges to see Gray's country churchyard. This, my friend told me, was where his father-in-law had for many years been the vicar. By providence or coincidence, his wife, mother-in-law and two grown-up kids turned up to tend the grave as we were leaving. A few weeks later, we went to Chichester to pay homage to the knight, his lady and the little dogs at their feet so ambiguously given another afterlife in Philip Larkin's 'An Arundel Tomb'.

This Sunday it was Little Gidding in Cambridgeshire, where Nicholas Ferrar and his extended family founded an Anglican community in the 17th century, producing manuscripts of bibles and metaphysical verse. The spare, calligraphically sinuous manuscript of George Herbert's 'The Temple' was copied out here by the daughters, perhaps under the poet's direction as he lay dying. The church is tiny, domestically intimate, and lit only by candles. It moved T.S. Eliot to write the last of his 'Four Quartets'.

As we fret about diesel and self-driving cars become ever more viable, motorcycling sticks us right back into the visceral here and now. There is no elsewhere – only that bend you have to commit to correctly, the road surface to assess, that overtake to nail. The beginning and end of a ride are not separated in the metallic parenthesis of car or train, but a thrillingly immediate narrative of place and feeling – like the best kind of poem. Maybe, as Eliot put it in 'Little Gidding', 'the intersection of the timeless moment/Is England and nowhere. Never and always.'

I can't tell you how quickly I went on the way back to Oxford, but those long, low-rise distribution centres around Milton Keynes that try unsuccessfully to slink into the landscape with their colours of sky and field barely registered at all. Byron next.

Notes on... Wet weather boots Laura Freeman

'*Foot – foot – foot – foot – sloggin' over Africa – / (Boots – boots – boots – boots – movin' up and down again!).*' I do like Rudyard Kipling. I know I'm not supposed to. Trigger warning: empire, jungle stereotypes, microaggressions against monkeys, cultural appropriation of other people's elephants. But what a stomping great marching poem 'Boots' is.

Learn at least the first verse by heart: it's the right rhythm for walking when the rain comes on and you're miles from home. *Boots–boots–boots–boots*. Imagine the dust stamped up from the veld. The other one to sing under your breath in a downpour is: 'She'll be comin' round the mountain (when she comes).' It rouses even the dampest spirits.

You can brave any weather with the right boots, and British boots are the best in the world. They must be waterproof. None of this rubbish about 'water-protected'. That's what shoe shops say about boots to get you from the front door to the bus stop. Fine for mizzle and a puddle, but not up to Sunday walks in the mire. You want the tough stuff: 'Gore-Tex', 'all-weather', 'rubber membrane'.

I learned the hard way. For a walking holiday on the Sussex Downs I pitched up in ten-year-old Russell & Bromleys. Soles, heels and laces replaced each time they wore thin. Never a crack in the leather. And, damn them, they leaked. Half an hour into the first morning, halfway up a hill. The first heart-sinking *squelch*. Then three hours' walking until lunch, socks soggier every step. Squelch – squelch – squelch – squelch – sloggin' over Eastbourne cliffs. That decided me. No more high-street lace-ups. I went to Clarks for the first time since nursery shoe-fittings, and bought a pair of Gore-Tex walkers. Stand ankle-deep in a fjord and not a drop gets through. They're not chic, though. For that, there's Dubarry. Founded in 1937, it celebrates its 80th birthday this year. There's something reassuring about Irish boots: proof against peat bogs. Not technically British, I know, but I've tested my pair against our native marshes and they are ark-tight. (You do, however, go skating on ice.)

The Princess of Wales wears Le Chameau wellingtons from Normandy, which is not very patriotic. Hunter wellies hold the royal warrant, though the sheen has been rubbed off by Glastonbury pouters and by cabinet ministers responding with money-no-object urgency to winter floods.

There is no greater misery or privation than cold, wet feet. Reading Thomas Hardy's *Tess of the D'Urbervilles* again last winter I thought: I can bear it. The assault, the baby, the little grave, abandoned on her honeymoon, the turnip farm. But when Mercy Chant takes Tess's boots hidden in the hedge to give to the poor… that was too much for me. Oh, Tessy!

Notes on... Book clubs Emily Rhodes

Everyone knows somebody who belongs to a book club. From informal gatherings of bookish friends in living rooms and cafés to ticketed events organised by newspapers, publishers and hubs like the Southbank Centre, and including rather more off-piste groups such as my own walking book club on Hampstead Heath, book clubs have become an integral part of our cultural landscape.

At first glance it's somewhat puzzling as to why they've become such a phenomenon. Surely it is surprising that readers, whom one assumes to be on the more introverted side of the spectrum – content to retire with a book of an evening rather than paint the town red – can be such keen talkers?

The act of reading is by necessity anti-social. It demands concentration, a zoning out of the wider world in order to take in the words on the page. This silent focus fosters an intense bond between reader and writer; hence the power of a

good book. We've all experienced this: both its physical effects – a sharp intake of breath, unbidden tears, involuntary snorts and chuckles – and the bruise of its emotional punch. Sometimes a book is too powerful to be contained in the intimate bond between reader and writer. Julian Barnes wrote in the *Guardian* about his experience of reading John Williams's *Stoner*: the 'joyful internal word-of-mouth that sends a reader hurrying from one page to the next… in turn leads to external word-of-mouth, the pressing of the book on friends, the ordering and sending of copies.' To this I would add: the overwhelming desire to talk about the book to someone else who's read it.

'Man is a social animal,' Aristotle pointed out. We instinctively like to share our experiences, and those undergone while reading a good book are no exception. Of course everyone in a book club has to have read the book, providing a vital common ground. It means that rather than enduring grim monologues, such as when a friend tells you about the bliss of her holiday when you've been stuck in the office for months, everyone can participate in an engaging exchange of ideas. Moreover, this commonality enables conversations between people who might otherwise be quite different, struggling to find much to say to one other past the dreaded 'So what do you do?'

So friendships bloom, and with this pleasure in words spoken comes a greater appreciation of words written. Here is a chance to discover a variety of opinions about a book, and an opportunity to develop our own ideas; book clubs encourage readers to give a book at least a fraction of the time and thought it deserves.

Sometimes I think of literature as a mighty castle – glorious to those who know and love it, but horribly intimidating to those who can't penetrate its defences. The portcullis falls ever lower as the welcoming ways in of bookshops and libraries dwindle. Book clubs extend a much-needed welcome to those who loiter outside, propping open the gate with every suggestion of a book to read, each opportunity for friendly discussion. They stop the castle from falling out of use, into nothing more than a crumbling, albeit beautiful, ruin.

Notes on... Pigeon racing Jon Day

Pigeon racing isn't much of a spectator sport. Race birds are driven to the 'liberation point', where they're released to fly back to their homes. Only the liberation and the return are witnessed – what happens in between is a mystery. This is partly what makes pigeon racing so fascinating. It's also what can make it so stressful.

In the summer of 2021, between 5,000 and 10,000 pigeons went missing during a race from Peterborough. Usually fanciers aren't too worried if a few birds don't make it straight home from a race; they'll rest up and return a few days later, no worse for wear. But this time the losses were exceptionally large. 'I have never heard of anything like this,' said Ian Evans, manager of the Royal Pigeon Racing Association. 'It is a real mystery.'

Racing pigeons are closely related to feral pigeons – themselves urban relatives of *Columba livia*, the rock dove – but have been selectively bred over thousands of years to have an unrivalled ability to find their way home. Quite how they do so isn't fully understood. There is some evidence that, like migratory songbirds, pigeons can detect the Earth's magnetic field (fanciers have speculated that the Peterborough losses might have been caused by a solar storm interfering with this mechanism; the Met Office says no unusual activity has been recorded). It also seems likely that they navigate using an 'olfactory gradient map', produced by smells carried on prevailing winds.

However it works, this homing ability has made pigeons one of our oldest companion species. They were used to break the sieges of Modena and Paris, and won awards for bravery during both world wars.

Pigeon racing was invented by Belgian coalminers at the end of the 19th century. The sport depended on two other things: the railways, which allowed fanciers to send their birds far from home for training, and mass-produced clocks, which enabled them to record their flying times accurately. For a time, pigeon racing was one of the most popular sports, by participation, in Europe. In Britain in the 1950s, half a million fanciers tended millions of birds.

Now, in the West at any rate, pigeon racing is in decline. This is partly reputational: the stock of the pigeon – so high in the post-war years, when they were seen as heroes – has plummeted. Some flyers blame an increase in the raptor population. Brexit, too, is having an effect. Fanciers have lobbied the government to end new animal health regulations which threaten to make cross-Channel racing impossible. In China and central Asia the sport is flourishing – last year a Chinese fancier paid a record £1.4 million for a champion Belgian bird named 'New Kim' – but in Britain pigeon racing has become very much a minority pursuit.

With luck, most of the missing Peterborough pigeons found their way home (I once lost a bird on a flight from Cambridge; he turned up, unruffled, six months later). But some might not have chosen to return at all. These will have joined their feral cousins on the streets of our towns and cities. Next time you pass a flock, you might see if you can spot one.

Notes on... Chinese porcelain Timothy Brook

Next time you're in a shop that sells Chinese blue and white porcelain, pick up a piece and turn it over. Chances are good it will carry an inscription in blue on the bottom. Called a reign mark, it tells you which emperor ruled when the piece was made. As the last reign ended in 1912, the dish you've picked up should logically be at least a century old. Hundred-year-old porcelain selling for £2? Not likely, but hold that thought.

When you buy a Chinese dish today, you are doing what collectors have done since porcelain started arriving in London in Elizabethan times. Shakespeare mentions this marvel in *Measure for Measure*, when Elbow's pregnant wife asks Mistress Overdone for stewed prunes. The brothel-keeper happens to have some in a threepenny dish, a fine dish but not, Shakespeare tells the audience, a 'China-dish'. Mistress Overdone runs a profitable business, but not even she can afford Chinese porcelain. Within a generation, such ware was an affordable luxury.

Our taste for blue and white ceramics started in Persia, where potters decorated their low fired wares with floral and abstract designs in cobalt blue. When Kublai Khan conquered China in the 13th century, he brought the Persian taste to China, and Chinese manufacturers responded. Having recently developed the technology to produce true porcelain, they outdid the Persians. Chinese blue-and-white dazzled buyers everywhere and monopolised the high end of the market.

When potters elsewhere started to make cheap substitutes, the potters in Jingdezhen – the porcelain capital of China – responded by designing showy blue and white porcelains to sell at the lower end of the market. This was the style Europeans encountered when they arrived in Asian waters in the 16th century. Chinese collectors scorned the stuff, but Europeans buyers were entranced. The profits on both sides of the wholesale trade were stunning. Dutch and Mexican potters immediately tried their hands at making plausible substitutes, but it would be a century before Josiah Wedgwood and others cracked the technical secrets. The old potters of Jingdezhen would surely be amused to know that low-end Wedgwood is now being produced in China.

Now look again at the reign mark on the bottom of that blue and white dish you picked up in the shop. If it reads Wanli, the emperor who ruled China when Shakespeare was alive, you could be holding porcelain four centuries old: very expensive. You could also be holding a Dutch copy of a Japanese copy of a Vietnamese copy of a Chinese copy of a Chinese original: less expensive. Most likely you are handling a knock-off made last month with no pretensions to do anything other than to please the eye. Sometimes only experts can tell the difference. My best advice is simply to buy what you like. No matter which blue-and-white you choose, you're buying into the same rich history.

Notes on... Hunting Camilla Swift

I hadn't jumped a single thing for almost ten years. This season, however, I am happily jumping hedges that my horse and I can't even see over the top of. Crazy? Probably. But when the adrenaline is pumping, and an inviting-looking hedge is looming directly in front of you – well, what's a girl to do?

The sheer joy of hunting comes from far more than just dressing up in a smart coat and shiny boots and drinking port. It's the simple pleasure of being out in the field, watching the hounds do what they do best, and enjoying the pure beauty of the sport. One of my favourite memories this season is of watching the hounds work through a field of leeks, the only sign that they were there being the little puffs of mist above the crop, and the odd head briefly popping up to double-check its whereabouts.

It's the thrill of clearing a 5 ft hedge without thinking twice (just kick on, find a nice-looking gap and pray, is my technique). 'How brave,' people say, looking at the photographs. 'I could never do that.' Well, I never thought I could, either. There may be photographic proof, but my memory has erased the details of the whole fearsome jump, a bit like it used to do with those shocking exam papers I knew I had failed. It's about jumping our way across Oxfordshire; discovering D-day training sites scattered with replicas of Normandy's Atlantic Wall, and the true location of James Bond's *Skyfall* (sadly, in the film it's Surrey rather than a remote Highland glen). Those are the little things that make a day perfect.

To a certain extent it's just the rush of it all, and I probably am an adrenaline junkie of the worst kind. Galloping across country at high speeds may not be the most sensible thing to do, but somehow all thoughts of sanity disappear when the field master takes off. The feeling of being at one with the horse; an animal that, however good a hunter it may be, never leaves you quite sure what it might do next, is one that simply can't be matched. Why would I put my life into the hands of an immature, six-year-old Irish gelding? There's only one answer: I must be mad.

I only hunted once before the ban on foxhunting came into force in 2005. My father, being the kind of person that he is, decided that if Blair's hunting legislation was going to be enacted, the least we could do was lend some support. So off we went on a pair of hirelings; me aboard a tiny Exmoor pony, and him on something that should really have been pulling a brewer's dray. Today, I'm out hunting every weekend, and any other day that I possibly can – and I'm far from the only one. Since the ban, the number of people who hunt regularly has grown to around 45,000 – an increase of 5,000. And if their experience is anything like mine, who can blame them?

Notes on... Country house opera
Guy Dammann

I stole a blanket the other night. Rather a nice one, in fact. I feel bad about it, of course, but guilt is less inconvenient than pneumonia; and after trying to blow-dry my waterlogged dinner jacket with the winds howling through Garsington Opera's 'airy' pavilion, it seemed like pneumonia or the blanket were the options.

Forgive the melodramatic, self-justificatory tone. That, too, has its roots in the evening's diversions, which included a performance of *Intermezzo*, Richard Strauss's melodramatic and self-justificatory autobiographical account of a marital misunderstanding. It's an odd piece, lovely in some ways, trite and misogynistic in others.

Some decades ago, after a May Day ball in Oxford, I learned that poncing around wet and muddy fields in evening dress is misguided; a category error, even. I vowed not to do it again. But now my early summer is occupied with little else than poncing around wet fields in evening wear. Garsington, Glyndebourne, Grange Park – and that's just the home counties. I can now find challenges for my dry-cleaner much further afield, in Longborough, Iford or Bampton.

Country house opera suits opera critics because the levels of invention and talent are commonly very high, despite meagre resources. It also suits the British public, who, though they remain uncomfortable around opera, certainly feel at home with boozy picnics in questionable weather.

But you needn't stay in Britain for summertime opera. You may even travel to countries where they have a summer. Coincidentally, some of those countries are entirely comfortable with the idea of opera, so there's no need for picnics. In Salzburg, for example, going to the opera is both natural and desirable. The festival puts out a red carpet on opening nights. There are even paparazzi, though God knows where they send the photographs. A more spectacular natural setting may be found in Bregenz, where the stage is lapped by the mountain-ringed Lake Constance and performances are only occasionally disrupted by James Bond types infiltrating fictional criminal networks. Across the border in Bavaria lies Bayreuth. Here the edifying spectacle of Wagner's operas – and the unedifying one of his feuding descendants – may be enjoyed in a tailor-made setting.

In Italy, the choice is equally rich, with wall-to-wall Puccini in Torre del Lago and more mixed fare flourishing in the adapted handball stadium that houses the Macerata Opera Festival. Americans, too, have grown comfortable around opera, though this may have less to do with the art of sung drama than with the coincidence that opera tickets remain an excellent way not only to tell others how much money you make, but also that you have a certain *je ne sais quoi*.

I'm sticking with the home counties. I have a blanket to return, after all.

Notes on... Garden sculpture
Prue Leith

Boris Johnson has three lifesize, carved wooden elephants in his garden, given to him by his wife for his 60th birthday. But here's a warning for them both: garden sculptures are horribly addictive. Once you have one, you want more – and most of the good ones are ridiculously expensive unless, like my husband and me, you improvise.

My husband John, who used to be a fashion designer and manufacturer, has taken to making iron sculptures, although he's too modest to call himself a sculptor. I draw stuff, he says, and Sked (Malcolm Sked, the local blacksmith) makes them. So far, John has created a huge wrought-iron pagoda with a floral explosion on top and two urns, one

containing a giant metal phormium whose rusty leaves glow red in the evening sun and wave in the wind. There's also a gigantic fantasy plant with spathe-like white flowers and enormous heart-shaped leaves growing out of an old truck wheel embedded in a block of Cotswold stone. This was immortalised on film when we were making *Prue Leith's Cotswold Kitchen*. Two weeks later a gale wrenched the 8ft leaves from the wheel and sent them flying across the garden. 'Ah,' said John, 'I meant to concrete them in. Bit of a rush job for the camera.'

Even before John took to DIY art, our garden sculpture collection was impressive.

My Cambodian daughter and I bought a two-ton Buddha in Siem Reap. The Buddha was made by stonemasons who are gradually replacing all the looted sculptures of Angkor Wat. When we first saw the statue, it was unfinished – the Buddha's face and shoulder exquisitely carved, with the rest of him still to emerge from the stone. It was magical. We offered full price for him as he was, but they wouldn't hear of anything so sacrilegious. They'd been making statues exactly like this for 500 years. Chastened, we bought the statue anyway and Mrs Johnson will sympathise with the cost of shipping.

My garden also boasts a life cast of an employee of the Royal Shakespeare Company, which was made as a figure in the background of a play set in a lunatic asylum. We bought him for £5 from the props department and when we carried him to the carpark, each holding him by an elbow, passers-by smiled sympathetically, thinking we were taking home a drunk, face down, knees bent, feet dragging.

The man was white, and when we sat him in our garden, on top of the compost heap, visitors would take fright, thinking he was a ghost, so I painted him all over with resin and graphite and now he looks like a bronze. A few summers back, birds nested in a hole in his head and, once the chicks had flown, I filled the head with fibreglass foam, which I squirted through the ear-hole. It swelled dramatically and bubbled out through the hole so now he has one cauliflower ear. He still looks great.

I hope one day to have one of Emily Young's huge female heads with windblown hair, or Sophie Rider's enormous Lady-Hares, or a water sculpture by William Pye. But until I win the lottery I'm going to have to make do with improvisation.

Notes on... Visitors books
Mary Killen

Two things come to mind when I think about visitors books. The first is the memory of leaving the home of a low-profile and secretive single man whose company is widely craved. I had been revelling in a sense of self-importance as I had good reason to suspect that the previous occupant of my guest bed had been none other than the late Queen Elizabeth II. Surely this proximity elevated my own moral and social status in some osmotic way? But when I suggested I sign his visitors book my host became querulous. He declared that he didn't have a visitors book for the precise reason that he didn't like the idea of his friends 'snooping' to see who else had been there.

I think of the canny businesswoman who ran a holiday cottage letting agency in Devon 20 years ago. Then, as now, chancers were trying it on vis à vis refunds. One complained that noisy building work had ruined his family's recent holiday. The canny businesswoman went directly to the visitors book where the family had written – as encouraged by the agency – an account of their stay.

A rave review was detailed there. The cosiness, the log fires, the happy days on the beach… No mention of noise. She photographed the pages and sent them back to the complainant. That was the last she heard from him.

But lengthy descriptions and compliments are not encouraged by grandees who keep visitors books for friends. They want only name and date. In fact they often enforce this by standing next to those signing. The reason for this diktat is that so many people get into a state trying to think of something witty or appropriate to say.

One of these enforcers is my friend Louise with whom, 30 years ago, I drove for miles to a bespoke paper-maker. Louise had learned that the pages, unless made of acid-free, archival-quality paper, would crumble to dust in 50 years or so and the historic social record would be of no value. The resulting leather-bound, 'landscape'-sized book, about half the size of a card table, has stood in her entrance hall all these years with a proper pen next to it.

Why do visitors books matter? I asked Louise (Guinness). 'The main point is the written record of who has spent a night in the house. You'd be surprised how often people say "I think it's about five years since I was last here" and you can say "Let's check the visitors book". It's also quite sweet seeing the handwriting of children develop from wonky, filling-up-half-a-page scratchings to their final adult scrawl over the years. It is also for the hosts a visible proof of some kind of achievement – you can flick through the year and think "Well, I did that weekend… oh and that one" and so on.'

Louise adds: 'I also have a bossy note, now laminated, that reads "Please don't SQUEEZE. If in doubt start a new page". This is a personal, perhaps very petty, preference as I think it looks awful to see a signature squashed at the end of a page. Sometimes shy people need encouragement to sign proudly and boldly.'

Incidentally, if you do have a royal to stay the custom is to give them a whole page, just for their own signature.

Notes on... Nominative determinism
Dot Wordsworth

In 2015, an orthopaedic surgeon called Limb, with three other doctors called Limb, wrote a paper on whether people's names were correlated with their medical specialties. The findings were striking.

In general surgery there were practitioners called Gore, Butcher, Boyle and Blunt. In cardiology, Hart and Pump. In anaesthesia there was a Payne but also a Painstil.

For the 313,445 entries in the medical register that they examined, the median frequency of names relevant to medicine was one in 149 – but in neurology, one in every 21 doctors had a name relevant to medicine. In genitourinary medicine, one in 52 had a relevant name. The authors admitted that specialties with the largest proportion of relevant names benefitted from the wide range of alternative English terms for the same anatomical parts and their functions, as in urology's Cox, Ball, Dick, Waterfall.

Limb et al were aware of an article on incontinence in the *British Journal of Urology* (1977), authored by Splatt and Weedon. It had featured at the beginning of a long series in the *New Scientist* that began in 1994. A letter to the magazine in that year from Professor C.R. Cavonius (1932–2003) seems to have first applied the term 'nominative determinism' to this phenomenon by which one's name is deemed to influence one's choice of occupation or personal characteristics.

Thus Walter Brain, the 1st Lord Brain, edited the learned journal *Brain* from 1954 to the day of his death in 1966. Igor Judge, who died in 2023, did become a judge, but was never known as Judge Judge, being Mr Justice Judge in the High Court. In 2023, Thetford was given a Bishop Bishop.

But the Conservative MP Michael Lord defied determinism in 2011 when he was ennobled, deliberately taking the title Lord Framlingham, not Lord Lord. Since 2020, the President of the Royal Horticultural Society has been Keith Weed; but he has been lots of other unweedy things, notably Unilever's chief marketing officer.

It is not that such correlations hadn't been noticed before. The American columnist Franklin P. Adams was credited with applying in 1920 a new term *aptronym* (an ill-formed word derived from *apt*-and-*nym*) to a name regarded as (humorously) appropriate to a person's profession or characteristics, such as Mr Glass the glazier Ho, ho.

It seems to me that this is close to the names in Happy Families, the card game invented by John Jaques in 1851. His families included Mr Bones the butcher, Mrs Bung

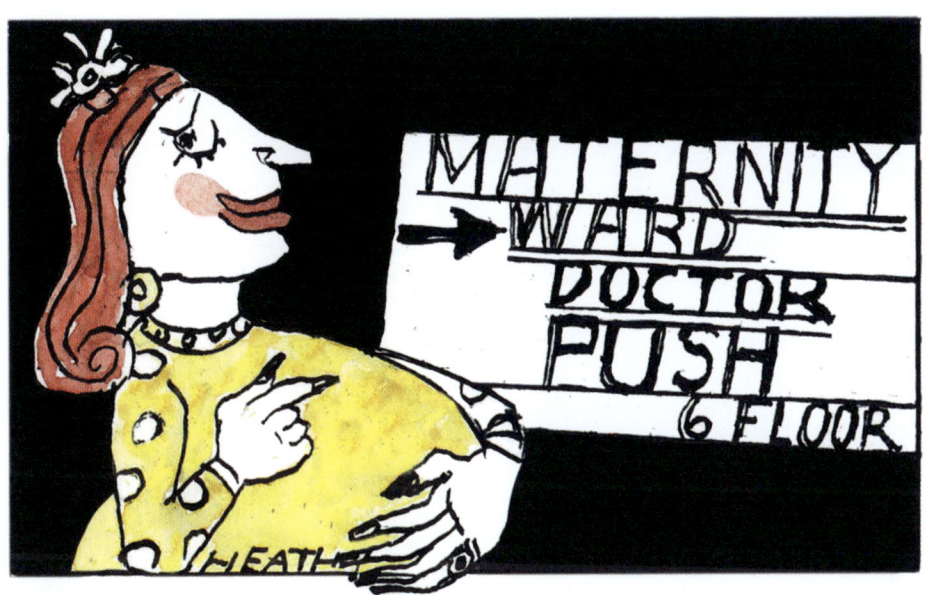

the brewer's wife, Master Grits the grocer's son and Miss Tape the tailor's daughter. This sort of denomination harks back to a convention of stage character names like those used by Ben Jonson: Sir Epicure Mammon the gourmand, Fly the potman. But that is different from a man called Fly growing up to become a potman. Detecting real-life nominative determinism often attracts confirmation bias: one disregards unrewarding examples.

A *Spectator* reader has pointed out the suitability of my name for my hobby of examining words. But it could not be a case of nominative determinism, for my maiden name was Blount – unless I fell for my husband attracted by his surname. That might explain a lot.

Notes on... Doner kebabs
Michael Simmons

I once shared a bed with a doner kebab. I'd hungrily joined a 3 a.m. queue for post-pub sustenance, only to pass out as soon as I sat down on my bed to eat it. It was a vinegary and leathery bedfellow to wake up to, but I've felt ever since that spending a full night with a doner qualifies me as an expert.

I can tell you that any major city's kebab purveyors can be ranked by the number of pints you need to have drunk before you feel like tucking in. Think of this number like the zones on the London Tube map. At the smart end there's the zone one kebab: restaurant-grade and easily enjoyed as part of a full sit-down meal. Some kebab shops won't even serve it, with one pretentious establishment deploring it on its menu: 'We do not sell doner kebabs. "doners" are made

from the cheapest, fattiest mince. At the other end there's zone six: a last resort on the way home from a six-pint (or more) pub session.

Each kebab house, whatever its zone, is run by a patriarch who is referred to as 'bossman' ('Cheers bossman, go easy on the garlic'). They oversee everything in their kebab kingdom, from the daily preparation of the carcass-sized kebab stacks – made by marinating lamb or beef and then layering it on to a vertical rotisserie machine – to flirting with the friendlier customers and acting as a bouncer to the nocturnal and usually inebriated clientele who provide most of bossman's business.

An important part of the doner-buying experience is the decor. One place I used to frequent in kebab zone six had a display of lemons that seemed fresh the first time I visited but thereafter never changed. When I moved house and came to say goodbye to the bossman, I took a close look at the lemons and saw that they were encapsulated in a thick layer of mould. My new – zone three – local has a display of seafood. Seeing the same beady black-pearl-eyed king prawn I saw the Saturday before gives me pause each week. I order anyway. They're just that good: savoury, salty, spicy, fatty sliced lamb, salad and sauce (mixed is a must) wrapped in a fluffy comfort-blanket flatbread. It's the greatest of all-time post-pub snacks.

Kebabs have been a staple of Ottoman cooking for centuries, but it was 1970s Berlin that birthed the doner. When post-war West Germany experienced its *Wirtschaftswunder* (economic miracle), a huge industrial ramping up needed thousands of migrant workers to take the jobs that couldn't be filled on account of the Wall cutting off the labour supply from the east. Turkey provided the answer and over 12 years 650,000 *Gastarbeiter* (guest workers) and their families settled in Germany, bringing the Ottoman vertical rotisserie cooking style with them.

Doner is a hot topic in Germany, where 1.3 billion are consumed every year. In 2024 the youth wing of the German Left party proposed an economic intervention of which their Soviet political antecedent would surely be proud. Doner kebab prices would be capped with £4 billion of annual state funding, ensuring everyone could get their hands on the perfect snack for under a fiver. One voter even confronted Chancellor Olaf Scholz about the cost of living with the words: 'Speak with Vladimir Putin… I'm paying €8 for a doner.'

Notes on... The speaking clock
Alan Steadman

Ask young people today if they know that they can dial a number to hear the time and you would probably be met with blank stares. Why would you pay to phone a speaking clock when the time is right there in front of you on your watch or phone screen?

However, if you were young in bygone days you may have memories of getting parental permission to phone 'TIM' and hear somebody telling the time… precisely. In fact, every year millions of people still phone this service – now the BT Speaking Clock – almost 90 years after its introduction.

It was launched by the Post Office on 24 July 1936 and was aimed at folk who did not have a clock or watch to hand. Before that you had to phone the exchange operator to settle any dispute as to what the correct

time was and, of course, mechanical timepieces were not always reliable. The Speaking Clock is a very accurate service indeed, to within five milliseconds (5/1000th of a second). Even Big Ben takes its time from it.

The service was originally accessed by dialling 846, which coincided with the letters T.I.M. – giving it its colloquial name. However, this code was only used on the telephone systems for the major cities. Other numbers were 952, followed by 80 and 8081 until it was standardised as 123 in the early 1990s. Calls to the Speaking Clock increase on four very time-sensitive days: as midnight approaches on New Year's Eve; when the clocks change in March and October; and on Remembrance Sunday for the two-minute silence.

Nowadays other services are available but the BT Speaking Clock remains an emblem of accuracy and one that still uses a *real* voice. The first 'golden voice' belonged to Ethel Jane Cain, an exchange operator for Croydon. Unfortunately a slight speech impediment was detected at the end of some sentences and apparently it took months to eradicate this from the glass discs on to which her voice was recorded. The other permanent voices have belonged to Pat Simmons 1963–1985; Brian Cobby 1985–2007; Sara Mendes da Costa 2007–2016; and, well… me.

I have had that privilege since 9 November 2016 after I entered and won a competition run by BT and the BBC for *Children in Need*. I have the first Scottish voice and, as is the trend these days, it is somewhat removed from the Received Pronunciation of previous ones.

The recordings took place over two sessions at the BT Tower in London and although the technology bore no resemblance to that in 1936, the script was remarkably similar. It was broken up into segments of hours, minutes and seconds and the well-known phrases of 'at the third stroke' and 'precisely' were of course still there.

Nine years on, I'm still asked for the time when out and about and I'm sure there are those who think that I tell the time, live, every day. I've been asked if I'm having a day off or if someone else is covering for me as I make my way round the supermarket. A personal favourite: 'This speaking clock job – what are the hours like?' It's even been suggested that my epitaph should read 'At the third stroke…'.

Notes on... Ferret racing Peter Krijgsman

The British are fond of ferrets. There is a portrait of Queen Elizabeth I at Hatfield House holding one on a collar and lead. For Yorkshire miners in the 1970s, tales of 'ferret-legging' – an endurance test whereby two ferrets were put down competitors' trousers – were legendary. (The world record is held by Frank Bartlett, a retired headmaster, who managed to endure the bites and scratches for five hours, 30 minutes.)

So it feels a little odd that ferret *racing* was invented in the United States. Rather than being conceived in the backroom of some raucous Jacobean tavern, it was a Friday night distraction for rednecks laying oil and gas pipes through the North American wilderness. Racing was also an after-work gig for the ferrets whose instinct to explore dark places made them quick and useful assistants for threading cables down pipes.

Today in Britain, there are several rent-a-ferret companies you can turn to if you want to set up a race. A race night will feature dozens of the animals running eight or ten contests over the course of a few hours, but the stakes are not high – usually £1 a time. Winning tickets share the total proceeds minus a cut for whatever cause is being sponsored.

In my tiny Somerset village of Huish Champflower we decided to hold our own ferret race for the first time. We erected a temporary bar which encouraged a good pre-race braggadocio: mock form-studying, loud predictions on outcomes and nonsensical betting strategies.

Five pipes were laid on the polished pine floor, each one a different colour, a box with a trap door at one end and an open exit at the other. The ferretman had recruited six children to lift the trap doors when he blew the starter's whistle. Some of them looked more capable of concentration than others, which should have given some runners an advantage, but made little difference.

Ferretman was an intriguing figure. Stocky and bow-legged, he came from Dulverton, bang in the centre of Exmoor, where everyone hunts, shoots, kills, skins, traps or catches something. I didn't count the number of fingers on each of his hands, but there did seem to be quite a few missing, with a lot of sticking plaster on the remaining ones. This lent weight to the one health and safety notice of the evening: should a ferret break loose and run past you, don't pick it up.

The races didn't take long and were only really interesting if you held a betting slip. The last raised the loudest roars as the ferrets reached the end of the pipe and then refused to scamper out – four legs on the floor at the end was the definition of victory. Around £500 changed hands over the night, including the bar and the sponsorship. A third of it went towards

maintenance of the village hall, but the bigger dividend was simply how much fun it was. There are no pubs, shops, schools or other social outlets in Huish Champflower, so village hall and church events are the only way to get local people together on chilly winter evenings.

And, for any who might frown upon meaningless distractions in these challenging times, they are educational events too. Who would have guessed looking at Good Queen Bess holding her ferret on a gilded leash, that the animals smell something rotten. Another reason not to pick one up.

Notes on... St Nicholas Mary Wellesley

For a heartwarming Christmas tale, look no further than the medieval legend of St Nicholas – a story of sex-trafficking, cannibalism and murder. The historical Nicholas is a hazy figure whose scant biography was embroidered in the Middle Ages. The 12th-century Norman poet Wace wrote a colourful account of his life. It opens with the story that has informed the modern Santa Claus. Nicholas, we are told, took pity on a man who had once been wealthy but had fallen into poverty. The man had three daughters. Things were desperate – the man concluded that the girls had to be sold into sexual slavery. Nicholas visited the man's house on three consecutive nights and each night threw gold in through an open window.

Some of the other stories in Wace's poem are decidedly more macabre; many involve the miraculous resurrection of children murdered or accidentally killed. One such is the Miracle of the Boiled Infant, in which a mother is so overjoyed at the news that Nicholas has been selected as the bishop that she rushes to church to hear Mass, leaving her baby in an earthen tub over a burning

fire. When the service is over, she suddenly remembers her mistake and rushes home to find the baby unharmed and happily playing with the bubbles in the boiling water.

In another story, a man on a pilgrimage to St Nicholas is murdered and dismembered by an innkeeper and thrown into vats of salted meat. The man miraculously wakes the next morning and greets the innkeeper, who responds: 'Good fellow… I killed you,/ Shattered your bones and salted your flesh./ Saint Nicholas to whom you are going/Is very powerful and full of succour.'

English versions of this miracle story are even more grisly. In the late-medieval *South English Legendary* the pilgrim becomes three clerks. There a butcher offers lodging to three clerks (for which read 'students'), before murdering them in the hope of stealing their money. On discovering the clerks are broke, his wife recommends dismembering their bodies, grinding up their flesh and salting it for use in pies. Later St Nicholas appears as the couple are selling their pastries; the clerks miraculously come back to life; the butcher and his wife are moved to contrition. There are several things that are weird about this story, but probably no more weird than the story of a man travelling the world on a reindeer conveyance and sneaking into the bedrooms of sleeping children.

Modern Christmas traditions involve the wholesale deception of children. Our medieval counterparts, by contrast, saw the feast of St Nicholas as a moment to surrender power to them. In many English cathedrals, abbeys, churches and schools, the feast (6 December) was the beginning of a boy bishop's term of office. In an atmosphere of misrule that seems to pervade when the days are short and the nights long, a young choirboy would be appointed 'bishop' until Holy Innocents' Day (28 December). During his tenure he would dress in robes, preside at services, preach a sermon, and lead a procession through the streets during which a collection would be taken. The practice, like so many mad and wonderful traditions, was outlawed by Henry VIII.

Notes on... Friday 13th
Fergus Butler-Gallie

Uzeste contains 387 people and a dead pope. The tiny French village is one of the less glamorous papal resting places, where the earthly remnants of the unfortunate Clement V await the General Resurrection. How much of Clement is left is hard to tell. As his body lay in state after he died in 1314, the church was struck by lightning, causing a fire that consumed his corpse. The medieval mind assumed that this was an earthly metaphor for the eternal flames that consumed Clement in Hell.

Many identify this unfortunate pontiff as the first victim of the Curse of de Molay. Clement, a particularly craven occupant of the see of Peter, had moved the papacy to Avignon on the orders of the French king Philip IV, who then proceeded to co-opt him into his campaign against the Templar Order.

The Knights Templar were initially a military organisation formed with the aim of protecting pilgrims to the Holy Land. Soon, however, they had grown into a pan-European behemoth. This change of status brought enemies. King Philip in particular hated the Templars, desiring, it is said, their power and their money for himself. After the death of their protector, the previous pope, he moved quickly, with Clement's connivance. A date was set for mass arrests across France, with Templars from Grand Master Jacques de Molay downwards seized and charged with trumped-up claims of corruption, heresy and sodomy. Many of them – de Molay included – would later be burnt at the stake. The date set for the arrests was Friday 13 October 1307.

The rapid subsequent deaths of Clement, then Philip and then, within, appropriately, 13 years, the whole of his dynasty, set those fertile medieval minds whirring again. Had the order cursed the date of their arrest forever? Fridays were considered a day with particular power, being the day of the Crucifixion. Thirteen already suffered the concomitant association with Judas, the 13th person to take his seat at the Last Supper. Even before Philip's plot, Friday 13th seemed destined to be a day associated with bad luck. So it became, apart from in Italy, where Friday 17th is unlucky instead, due to its Roman numerals – XVII – being an anagram of *vixi*, Latin for 'I have lived'.

Italians aside, the superstition persists, even among those not suffering from the medicalised fear of Friday 13th: paraskevidekatriaphobia. An infamous *British Medical Journal* study in the 1990s found that the chances of being involved in

a traffic accident on the M25 on a Friday 13th compared with the rest of the year 'could be increased by as much as 52 per cent'. In the subsequent newspaper panic, the researchers insisted that their findings were 'tongue in cheek' and that people shouldn't change their plans on Friday 13th. Unless, of course, what you have planned is the mass arrest of the Knights Templar.

It is strange that a date can link those frazzled remains found in Uzeste to the traffic patterns of the M25 in the late 20th century. But that's the rather wonderful thing about superstition: it doesn't make sense at all.

Notes on... Squatting Julie Bindel

Since my squatting experience back in the 1980s, the practice has gone somewhat out of fashion. Squatting laws in the UK have become much stricter, and eviction by police and landlords is easier. Spanish squatters have it relatively good at the moment, with criminal gangs targeting second homes in Spain, claiming to be homeless and using their young children to make eviction far more difficult.

I recall my time squatting in a large, ramshackle terraced house in Surrey Docks, south London, when I first moved to London from Yorkshire. I was in my early twenties, claiming benefits, doing political activism, with no bank account or savings and I urgently needed somewhere to live.

The squat had been advertised in the window of the radical bookstore in Brixton. 'Lesbian? Feminist? No boy children? Need

a place to live? Low income? Vegetarian/vegan? A room in a large, comfortable squat with other like-minded women is available. Pets welcome.'

I went for an interview, and reassured them that I was vegetarian and that I didn't have noisy, drunken parties. I also agreed to the rules of no male visitors. I explained that the male members of my family lived in the North-East and that I had no male friends to speak of. In reality, I would have been deeply ashamed for my brothers or father to come anywhere near the place. We used paraffin lamps, there were mice and for electricity we had to plug into the nearest lamppost. My bedroom was freezing, the window didn't lock and I soon started looking for somewhere else.

I had also lied about not liking raucous evenings of drink and debauchery: my girlfriend would come round after work with cans of Heineken and a couple of bags of chips. We would watch women's prison dramas on my old black-and-white TV, laugh uproariously, and when the lager ran out, would go to the local kebab shop and buy double-priced under-the-counter booze (the licensing laws were much stricter in those days and you were not allowed to purchase alcohol after 10 p.m.).

One night, the kebab shop was closed. I managed to break into my housemate's bedroom (she was away) and stole her bottle of Advocaat because there was no other booze in the house. When she returned and found it gone, she went berserk.

The following week, a friend came round to dinner and, being Jewish, insisted on a Friday night meal. I bought a kosher chicken, thinking that no one would find out as both housemates were away for the weekend. Afterwards, I gave the kitchen a forensic clean, but unfortunately, I forgot to empty the bin before my housemates returned. The chicken carcass was nestling under the empty Heineken cans.

I was given my marching orders. Thankfully, my girlfriend, a carnivore who loved late-night shenanigans, asked me to move in with her. Reader, that was 34 years ago, and we are still together. That chicken carcass has a lot to answer for.

Notes on... Lonely hearts ads
Anthony Whitehead

Published in Britain for at least 330 years, lonely hearts ads are now a rare sight – driven to the brink of extinction by the rise of dating apps.

This is a pity. 'The personals' were a voyeur's delight. Even if you weren't looking for love, you still read them. They could be tragic, comic, or both – like this one placed in an 1832 edition of the *Dorset County Chronicle*: 'My wife has been dead 12 months ago, last Shroton Fair. I want a good steady woman for a wife. I do not want a second family. I want a woman to look after the pigs while I am out at work.'

His was a straightforward request, clearly stated. But quite often the ads were keyholes through which whole melodramas might be glimpsed. In 1788, the *Hibernian Telegraph* carried an ad placed by an elderly man who wished to marry 'a healthy pregnant widow' in order, he went on to explain, to disinherit a nephew who had behaved 'in a manner unpardonable'.

Whatever the individual's situation, the goal was always the same: to find the right person. Today's apps do this by means of filters via which you can choose age, hair colour, income, etc. No doubt this is effective in its way.

Anyone, though, can fill in an online form and let the algorithm do its work. The harder task for the writer of a printed ad was to distil their hopes and dreams into just a few lines.

Some of the most entertaining lonely hearts are those which, instead of merely claiming a 'GSOH', actually have a go at displaying one, as in: 'Good looking, athletic, movie star millionaire seeks gullible stunner.'

Publications naturally attracted ads formed in their own image, so the 'Eye Love' column in *Private Eye*, for example, tended to specialise in the pithy: 'Have penis – will travel.' (That was the whole ad.) Another ended: 'No vicious spinsters!' And there was a whole sub-genre of humorous personals that riffed on the idea that, if you needed to place an ad at all, then you must be a hopeless loser: 'Tell me I'm pretty, then watch me cling,' warned one woman in the *London Review of Books*.

As Francesca Beauman points out in her history of the lonely heart, *Shapely Ankle Preferr'd*, publishers were well aware of how entertaining lonely hearts could be. She suggests that the man who, in 1786, advertised in the *Times* for a female companion to help him with 'an incurable weakness in the knees occasioned by the kick of an Ostrich', may have been made up by editors to keep the general readership entertained. The fact that personal ads sold papers was also not lost on the lady who later asked in hers: 'Why are we writing magazine copy for them?'

While many lonely hearts amused, others reflected the desperate times in which they were written. This 1915 ad still has the power

to shock: 'Lady, fiancé killed, will gladly marry officer totally blinded or otherwise incapacitated by the War.'

Discussing this ad in a letter to her own fiancé, Vera Brittain speculated that the woman did 'not want to face the dreariness of an unattached old-maidenhood'. But then, of course, the ad was not meant for her. Suitable gentlemen might have discerned other motives at play, including a noble sense of Christian or patriotic duty, sympathy, or simple niceness.

Brittain wondered if the lady received any replies. My guess is she got a sackful.

Notes on... Metal detecting
Nigel Richardson

Some detectorists will tell you that the holy grail of metal detecting is a hoard of Roman coins or Anglo-Saxon jewellery. Others will point out – borrowing a line from the TV series *Detectorists* – that actually the holy grail of metal detecting is the Holy Grail. Since I took up metal detecting, last summer, I have tried to set myself more modest goals.

They can be summed up in some wise words spoken to me in a field in Wiltshire after I'd suffered a near-barren day (my only finds having been a musket ball and 'canslaw' – a shredded drinks can). 'A find is a bonus, a good find is a good bonus,' said my fellow detectorist with a consoling hand on my shoulder.

My companion could afford to be sanguine – he was none other than the great Dave Crisp, finder of the Frome Hoard of Roman coins (52,503 of them) in 2010 and a poster boy for metal detecting due to the exemplary way in which he alerted the archaeological authorities once he'd unearthed the hoard.

The day I went out with Dave on the North Wessex Downs he bagged another half-dozen 'Romans', scattered across a field where he reckoned there had been a camp. It was his 'permission' – land on which the owner permits you to detect – and he had taken me there to enable me to find my first Roman coin, a rite of passage for detectorists. In other words he had led the horse to water. But the horse was unable to drink – and now stood there long-faced; a parched, useless Dobbin.

This sense of failure – and envy of other detectorists' success – had become familiar to me in my fledgling detecting career. I had tried to fight it, I really had. But it would just pop up – most shamefully a few months earlier in a freshly cut field in Oxfordshire.

Muffled up despite the humidity, a man was detecting near me when he shouted out 'Hammered!' and performed a brief jig in the stubble, a mini-version of the 'gold dance' that detectorists are supposed to do when they find the ultimate precious metal. Finding a 'hammered' coin – handmade, usually medieval – is another yardstick by which detectorists measure themselves and needless to say I was yet to find one. So when I witnessed this performance I felt sick to the stomach.

My mood darkened further when the detectorist walked over and insisted on sharing the moment with me. Then he explained why it meant so much – he had spent the previous few months undergoing treatment for cancer. This was the first time in a long time he had been outdoors and it had paid off with a lovely little find. Life was not, after all, unrelenting misery.

Though he didn't know it, he showed me how to become a better person – as, unwittingly, did other detectorists. People

like wise old Dave Crisp and a blind chap called Dean, who lost his sight in adulthood but still has a detailed map of his bit of Romney Marsh in his head.

I do find stuff. I'm not a complete waste of space as a detectorist. But I have come to realise that metal detecting is not really about finding hoards or hammereds. At the risk of sounding cheesy, it's about digging out and prizing the best bits of yourself. Mind you, I've practised the gold dance just in case.

Notes on... Fringes Martha Gill

Fringes have in modern times been considered attractive – Bettie Page, Elizabeth Taylor, Jane Birkin, Kate Moss – so it is easy to forget the period we have been living through is something of an aberration. For most of history, cutting a fringe has tended to mark a woman out as odd, mad or suspicious. In the 1600s, conservative churches thought a fringe indicated you were on your way to committing a mortal sin. This was true even as late as the 1920s, which is why the fringe was key to the rebellious flapper bob. There are stories of parents suing hairdressers for giving their daughter this haircut in case it damaged her chances of marriage.

Those old fringe politics are back. Having a fringe nowadays says one of three things: break-up, breakdown or mutiny. You may not get a fringe in this spirit, but that does not matter. Haircuts simply reflect the culture around them. You cannot go about explaining your haircut to everyone you meet.

How did we get here? Here are some inflection points. Hannah Horvath's self-cut fringe in Lena Dunham's series *Girls*, which begins as an attempt to recreate Carey Mulligan's pixie hairdo and ends with a Middle Ages bowlcut. Claire's bob in *Fleabag*, which makes her look like a pencil. Michelle Obama's 2013 'bangs', which she later referred to as a midlife crisis: 'I couldn't get a sports car. They won't let me bungee jump. So instead, I cut my bangs.'

Somewhere around 2018, the fringe officially became a symbol of emotional turbulence. It says: impulse. It says: kitchen scissors in front of the bathroom mirror. It says: self-sabotage. It says: no, I did not get therapy. In fact, in the US, the 'therapy vs bangs' meme is so well-established that last year magazines were running articles like 'I got bangs but it's not a cry for help'.

At this point I want to produce a male equivalent to the female fringe, but it's hard to think of one. There are male hairdos that give out similar distress signals: the mullet, the break-up beard, the man bun, the dramatic moustache.

But none of these matches the fringe for its sheer impulsiveness and capacity for regret. To grow a complicated moustache, a man must be in a chaotic emotional state for several weeks, repeatedly rejecting chances to change his mind. If at some point he recovers, he can simply shave it off. Male 1990s boyband 'curtains' are back, apparently, but that's somehow different. Male fringes don't have the same baggage.

You might think you can escape fringe prejudice. You cannot. The American writer Kaitlyn Tiffany has compared cutting a fringe to Britney Spears's 2007 head-shaving incident. They feel liberating but put you in a box. They attempt to seize control only to lose it. They reject the judgment of the world only to invite it more strongly. Fringes are a haircut paradox.

Beware of haircuts that feel liberating. And most of all beware the fringe. Almost all on-screen 'bad haircuts' feature a fringe because there is just so much that can go wrong: short, pudding bowl, skewed, greasy. Fringes are dramatic, irreversible (at least for a month or two) and of all haircuts the most tempting to have a go at yourself. Most people don't suit a fringe, a fact normally only realised after the deed is done. Resist.

Notes on... Whistling Steve Morris

There was, at least until recently, an old sign round the back of the Savoy banning whistling by staff or tradesmen. Whistling, it seems, can wind up some people. Winston Churchill hated the practice. Posters were put up in the War Rooms forbidding it. One day, on his way to Downing Street, he heard a paperboy whistling and sharply told him to stop it at once. The boy had some spirit and argued back: 'Why should I, you can shut your ears can't you?'

Churchill found this amusing – even if he never learned to love whistling. If he'd lived in my house, he'd have seen it differently.

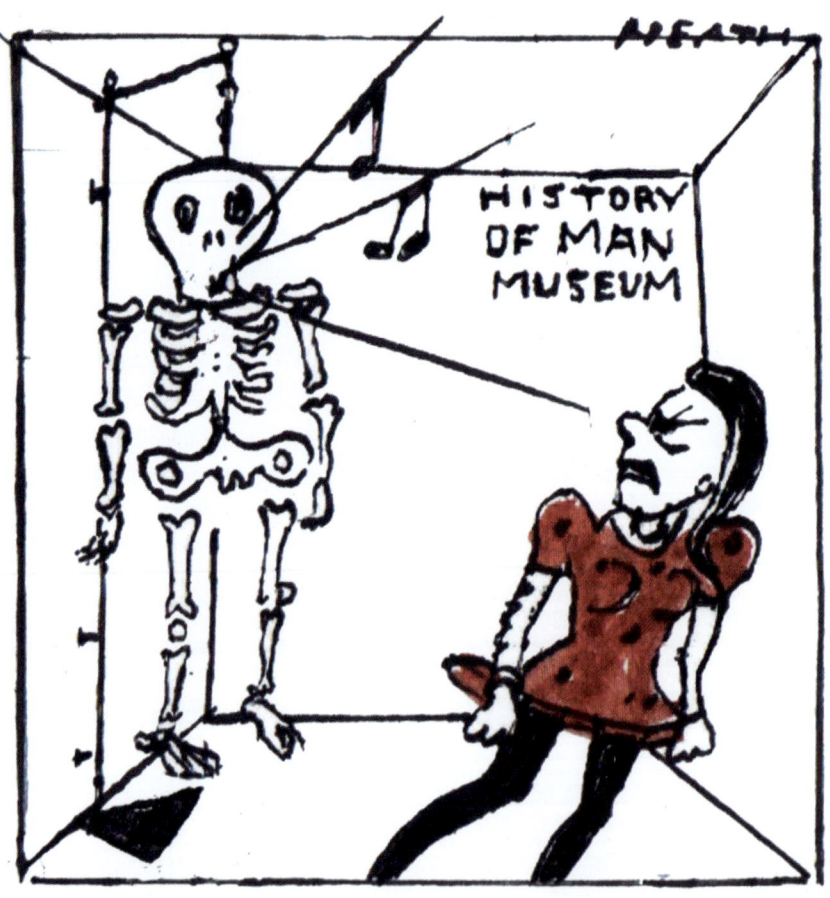

When I was growing up in the 1960s and 1970s, men – and it generally was men – seemed always to be whistling. It was the alternative soundtrack of my early life. But the whistles have gone quiet. I heard my postman whistling the other week and I realised I hadn't heard that sound for a very long time.

Whistling can be used for nefarious purposes. In the 19th century, pickpockets used coded whistles to warn when the Beadles were approaching. Upmarket shopping places like the Burlington Arcade in London banned whistling altogether, and it still stays that way.

But really there was no stopping the whistling craze and it took hold in working-class culture. It was both an act of defiance and also a shrug at life's vicissitudes.

In the late 19th century and well into the 20th, whistling was big business. The music halls and vaudeville palaces featured many whistlers who would perform tunes, bird song and yodelling. Ronnie Ronalde became a million-selling artist with his whistling songs. But his career is a sobering reminder of the impending silence of the whistle. In 1949 he played to a sell-out crowd of 6,000 people nightly at NYC's Radio City. The run lasted for ten weeks. He did his final show at the Beccles Public Hall & Theatre (capacity: 175) on 19 May 2013.

There have been some outlandish claims for the benefits of whistling. Pinocchio's Jiminy Cricket hails it as a cure for moral failing ('Take the straight the narrow path and if you start to slide – give a little whistle'). But John Lucas, author of *A Brief History of Whistling*, says: 'Whistling is about feeling at ease with yourself; there's sheer pleasure in hearing the sound of your own whistle.'

Whistling (or, at least, whistling well) is harder than it appears. Personally, I have never been able to whistle a note. The sound is produced by an interaction of lips, tongue, epiglottis, and sometimes fingers. It's all about creating air turbulence, something men are generally pretty great at.

But when it's good it is an art form, and a uniquely working-class one at that. We need a revival of whistling – not wolf-whistles, but musical whistling. Doctors report it is a great stress reliver and helps expand the capacity of the lungs. It is a way of laughing – or whistling – in the face of disaster too. 'Never try to shut up a whistler,' John Lucas tells me. 'It's part of the human spirit.'

Notes on... Tiramisu Tanya Gold

You can get drunk on tiramisu. I have done it. It takes two portions at least. You drink (I mean eat) the Marsala wine and the rum – and then must be escorted, tenderly, to the bus stop. I don't usually drink alcohol. If I did, I would smash up restaurants. But I do eat tiramisu. You have to eat a lot of tiramisu to be hospitalised. That is my reasoning.

Tiramisu means 'lift me up'. Like Caesar salad and the world, it has a detailed creation myth with its own pretenders, factions, expert witnesses and conspiracy theories. There is a website, the Tiramisu Academy, devoted to the mystery of its origin. ('Since 2011 we have been transmitting the culture of tiramisu.') The academy suggests tiramisu was invented to inspire men meeting prostitutes in 19th-century Treviso: an early Viagra for clients who took a dose when leaving the brothel, so they could then copulate with their wives. This sounds plausible – an Italian equivalent of 'my wife needs me to eat the last Quality Street toffee penny for sex'. The academy's expert witness, the writer Giovanni Comisso, who remembered his grandmother's personalised tiramisu, died in 1969.

The alternative narrative is that it was invented in Ado Campeol's restaurant Alle Beccherie in Treviso in 1969 – the year Comisso died – by Campeol, his wife Alba and the chef Roberto Linguanotto, who is the Perkin Warbeck figure in this drama. In this telling it was either a lucky mistake – Linguanotto dropped mascarpone cheese into the mixture for vanilla ice cream in error – or a palliative for aching nipples and an aching heart.

Sugar, cheese and biscuits were Alba's chosen foods to console her for the exhaustion she felt while breastfeeding her son Carlo; with Linguanotto she combined them. (The hard alcohol came later.) Campeol died in 2021 with his title 'the father of tiramisu' intact. This feels depressingly patriarchal.

Some things are worth a battle. The alchemy in tiramisu is just that. There are three distinct flavours (coffee, sugar, hard alcohol) and three textures (cream, crumble,

wet). When done properly, it is the greatest pudding there is. You can't get high on a profiterole, though I have tried, and you can only get low on treacle sponge. When done badly, it is repulsive: ladyfingers in cheap booze; something found at the bottom of a sink. It must be firm, not soggy. The cheese must be light, not heavy. The best I had was in Venice, at Muro Frari. The worst was in Camden Town in a restaurant that I hope has burnt down.

There are variations, but I am a purist (though we must have hard alcohol). Can I say I really hate panettone? And that Tia Maria does not belong anywhere outside of a slur? And that vodka should only ever be drunk neat, and not inside food? You may say it's just a trifle. Bah!

Notes on... Rude place names
Hannah Tomes

In the autumn of 2021, a gentle Norfolk waterway got into trouble with Facebook. The problem was its name – Cockshoot Dyke. Facebook's relentless algorithms blocked posts that mentioned the dyke and issued notifications warning about 'sexual content' and 'violence'.

The name of this stretch of water isn't, of course, actually rude at all. It relates to a fowl-hunting term for a broad glade through which woodcock might fly. The joy of supposedly 'rude' place names lies in their innocence. The village of Upperthong, near Huddersfield, is named after the Old English words *uferra* (upper) and *thwang* (a narrow strip of land), while Twatt in Orkney comes from the Old Norse *þveit*, meaning 'small piece of land'.

I've always felt some affinity for places with unusual names. I grew up in a tiny Shropshire village called Clunton (one letter from trouble). People would often ask me to repeat myself when I told them where I lived, thinking they'd misheard. Residents of the nearby and charmingly named Hopton Wafers never suffered such embarrassment, but I wouldn't have had it any other way. Only a Puritan – or a Facebook algorithm – wouldn't snigger at Pett Bottom, Ugley, Titty Ho, Low Cock How or Wetwang.

A few years ago, a man called Paul Taylor set off on a 1,800-mile moped journey across England and Scotland, visiting the places with the 'rudest' names to raise money in memory of a friend of his who had died of cancer. He started his journey in Shitterton, a hamlet near Bere Regis in Dorset, and set off for Twatt, taking in places such as Brawl (in Scotland), Sandy Balls holiday village (in Hampshire) and ending at the village of Bell End in Worcestershire. After reaching Twatt, Mr Taylor's Tomos XL 45 classic – top speed 28mph – suffered engine failure on a remote mountain pass. He completed the journey in a hire car, adding a few extra stops.

In the case of some of these place names, the etymology is up for debate. The village of Pity Me near Durham is said to have got its name after St Cuthbert's coffin was dropped by the monks carrying it, prompting the saint to scold them with the phrase from beyond the grave. Other theories suggest it may be a shortened version of the Norman-French Petit Mere, referring to a shallow lake or mere, or perhaps it's a play on the settlement's desolate character. Booze, a hamlet in North Yorkshire that is, ironically, without a pub, is thought to come from the Old English words for house (*hus*) and bow (*boga*), meaning 'the house by the bow' – possibly a reference to the curved hill on which it's situated. Wetwang either comes from the Old Norse *vaett-vangr*, 'field for the trial of a legal action', or derives from 'wet field', to distinguish it from a nearby dry field at Driffield.

Britain isn't alone. Dull in Perth and Kinross is grouped with Boring in Oregon and Bland in New South Wales. Hell in Michigan is said to have got its name when George Reeves, who helped form the town in the 1830s, was asked what it should be called and replied: 'I don't know, you can call it Hell for all I care,' and was taken at his word. And if you get tired of Hell, the state also holds a community called Paradise.

Notes on... Treehouses Andrew Watts

You can't (and probably shouldn't) *design* a treehouse. Treehouses should grow organically, in every sense: they must be made of wood, obviously – one definition of a treehouse is that it is a tree holding its dead friend – and the footings for the platform must be the knots or branches that are footholds when climbing the tree. Besides, it is only when you are halfway through building that you can work out where you need to fit round branches and add noggins – unless you build it between the trunks of

two separate trees, or use some sort of 3D mapping software, both of which sound very much like cheating.

So there wasn't any masterplan behind my son's treehouse. I bought some 2x4s in the first lockdown – timber merchants were the only shops open – and fitted them together in my head and the tree. My son had his own amendments (he thought that there should be a rope ladder he could raise and a trap door he could shut to escape from his enemies, which seemed like a very sensible precaution) and I had mine.

I had vaguely thought about making the walls from shiplap or featheredge but my wife pointed out it would look like a shed rather than a treehouse, and the boy was at least 30 years too young to be excited by a shed. Instead I found semi-circular rails, like the ones used to fence horse paddocks, on sale in an agricultural cooperative and screwed them next to each other with carriage bolts. And because the treehouse had never been designed – had never even been sketched out on paper – it was only when it was complete that I realised where I had seen that design before. It was the birthday cake that my mother always made for me as a child – a chocolate fort with chocolate fingers lining the outside.

I think what I am saying is that treehouses have a special place in our unconscious. I was always envious of children who had one when I was growing up – my parents' largest tree was a silver birch, which could only just cope with a birdhouse – but I could never say why. Nor why, on my first look round the house my wife and I eventually bought, the first thing I noticed was the mature tree in the garden with its capability for improvements; nor why, when it was finally erected, every child who visits excitedly runs to investigate.

Literary critics, trying to explain why so many children's books are set in treehouses, talk about liminality: living in a tree you are on the boundary of things, in the air but connected to the earth, close to the wildness of the woods but near enough to the house to call for help if the trapdoor lands on your fingers. It is a safe form of wildness.

But I suspect it goes deeper than that: perhaps even as deep as a primeval memory of our arboreal ancestors. Psychologists talk about prospect-and-refuge theory, the idea that we have evolved to desire places that give us a protected view over our world, whether it's the Serengeti or your father's lawn. My son's treehouse is the perfect example: every prospect pleases, but is a well-hidden refuge, being painted green to camouflage it from his enemies. I have never asked him who these potential enemies are. Mostly because I suspect it is his mother and me. Which is just as it should be.

Notes on... Aquariums Robert Porter

Fish tanks were probably first conceived in the distant past by the Chinese, but in many respects, aquariums are a distinctly British phenomenon. The first public one opened at Regent's Park Zoological Gardens in 1853. The word itself seems to have been first used in Philip Gosse's 1854 book *The Aquarium: An Unveiling of the Wonders of the Deep Sea*. And the glass-fronted version was patented by Edward Edwards in 1858. All that Victorian ingenuity definitely benefitted our underwater cousins.

It's hard to determine if keeping fish is trendy. On the one hand, there's not much to be said for goldfish in a bowl; on the other, a James Bond-style mega aquarium with sharks sends a thrill down the spine. When I was researching my book *For the Love of Fish: An Aquarist's Journey*, most people declared they weren't interested. But this aquarium-denial has its limitations: a recent survey concluded that 14 per cent of UK households (around four million) keep fish.

Some aquarists are keen on having the most difficult fish they can, migrating as soon as possible to cichlids and marine specimens. I have never understood that. One of the hardiest fish around – the zebra danio (or zebrafish) – is to my mind also one of the most beautiful, shimmering with silver and azure stripes. Moreover, the zebra danio has a significant place in scientific research and has even done a stint on the International Space Station.

The joys of fishkeeping are myriad. Not only do you experience the treat of fish of all shapes and hues, you also learn technical water chemistry around ammonia, nitrite and nitrate, and the disciplines of zoology and ichthyology. On top of that, the fishkeeping community is particularly friendly. Aquarists are more than happy to share knowledge. You might imagine an obsessive, eccentric bunch, but they are quite approachable.

Another joy is aquarists' propensity for creating naturalistic biotopes of, say, Amazonian habitats. This has the benefit of assisting conservation by preserving fish species, much as rare animals are protected in a zoo. There are those who might argue that this is contrary to nature, but on the whole they have not yet set their sights on aquarists.

That day may come, however. Most fish are vertebrates, and so benefit from the Animal Welfare Act 2006. Accordingly, it may be presumed they can feel pleasure, fear and pain. Did you know that if you abuse your fish, your tank could be seized by the authorities?

The hardest moment for any aquarist occurs at the beginning of the journey. When you establish a new tank, it takes weeks for bacteria to grow in the filter so they can process the ammonia excreted by the fish and turn it into nitrite and ultimately less harmful nitrate. This is known as tank cycling, and if not done right

can lead to your fish dying from ammonia or nitrite poisoning.

Many choose zebra danios for these early stages, because of their toughness. Once cycling is complete, though, the zebrafish are often replaced by seemingly more exotic specimens. That choice is, to my mind, an abomination. Make a long-term place for a shoal of zebra danios, and they will repay you a hundredfold.

Notes on... Black tie Harry Mount

Men don't look good in black tie. They might think that they look like Sean Connery in *Dr No*, but they end up looking like David Brent at the Wernham-Hogg annual Christmas do.

Black tie doesn't lend parties glamour; it just makes them depressing. The one good thing about black tie is that it is an invariably reliable pointer to a terrible evening.

Agonising teenage balls, with adolescents clashing braces in dark corners? Black tie. Boorish sports club dinners at university? Black tie. Prize-giving evenings in cavernous hotel ballrooms? Black tie. Business conventions with an after-dinner speech by Jeffrey Archer? Black tie.

The words 'black tie' on an invitation hope to raise the spirits with suggestions of luxury and class. In fact, they promise warm, acrid champagne, industrial quantities of hors d'oeuvres and a sickly, hollow feeling at the end of the evening.

The faults of black tie were built into the costume from the beginning. Black tie is the centaur of men's clothes – the ungainly meeting point of two sartorial animals who have never got on. In about 1885, that old dandy Edward VII swapped his tailcoat for a blue silk smoking jacket with matching trousers, made by Henry Poole of Savile Row. It was a relaxed alternative at Sandringham to the formality of evening tails. It was Edward VII's inspired relaxation of 19th-century fashions that led to the genius of today's everyday suits. The problem with the evening version – which eventually morphed into black tie – is that it clung on to some of the formal accoutrements of tails.

The shirt's winged collar survived from the evening tails look. So did the bow tie, a descendant of Beau Brummell's early-19th-century cravat. You ended up with an outfit that pulled in two directions: one looking forwards to the relaxed 20th century, the other back to the fogeyish 1800s.

The collision is even uglier when extra formalities are piled on top: frothy or slatted shirts, shirt studs and, God save us, the cummerbund, borrowed by British military officers from Indian fashion in empire days.

It all becomes completely unbearable when this half-formal mermaid of an outfit is clumsily lightened up with a splash of colour. Remember those terrible novelty white shirts with garishly coloured arms popular with Sloanes in the late 1980s? The arms stayed mercifully hidden until the Sloanes ripped off their dinner jackets after dinner, to boogie to 'I Will Survive'. Fortunately those shirts are long gone, but people still try to cheer up black tie with brightly coloured bow ties. That doesn't work, either.

As for the white dinner jacket, let's just pass over it in mournful, unrespectful silence. No one since Elvis has pulled off a white suit. Why should a white jacket with black trousers look any better? Barry Manilow? I rest my case.

In fact, the only time black tie works is when the bow tie is removed altogether – and then only because the dinner jacket and trousers come closest to looking like that sublime creation, the traditional British suit.

Partygoers of the world, unite! Get rid of black tie now! You have nothing to lose but your dickie bows.

Notes on... Hedgehogs Tom Holland

No wild animal is closer to the hearts of the British than the hedgehog. In poll after poll, it has been voted our favourite mammal. This is hardly surprising. Hedgehogs naturally inspire affection. Mrs Tiggy-Winkle, the companionable washerwoman created by Beatrix Potter, is only the most celebrated of a whole host of them who trot and snuffle through our national imagination. They are familiar to us in a way that few other wild creatures are. They can be met in fields and gardens, in hedgerows and parks. To see one is to feel the tug of a fascination with the natural world as a whole. In the words of Hugh Warwick, the naturalist who serves hedgehogs as their great contemporary champion: 'These are precious creatures to be treated with great respect.'

Over recent decades, however, we have not been treating them with great respect. An animal that was once ubiquitous seems on the brink of extinction. The most recent survey of hedgehog numbers in Britain was widely reported as good news. This was on the basis that populations in towns and cities seem to have stabilised, or perhaps even to be recovering. But beyond built-up areas hedgehog numbers continue to plummet. In certain parts of the country – East Anglia most notably – the population decline since 2000 has been 75 per cent. Since the second world war, Warwick estimates, it has been 90–95 per cent. Children are growing up who may never see a hedgehog in their entire lives.

It is not sentimentality to mourn this. Hedgehogs are precious in and of themselves; but they are also precious as bellwethers. A countryside unable to sustain hedgehogs is a countryside that is sick. It is no coincidence that the decline in their numbers should have begun during the second world war, when agriculture was expanded on an industrial scale. It is no coincidence either that this rate of decline should have accelerated since 2000. Hedgehogs cannot survive without the large numbers of invertebrates that are sustained by a healthy countryside. As insects decline, so inevitably do hedgehogs. Nor, when the average male likes to travel two to three kilometres a night, can their populations flourish if their habitats are sliced and diced by roads. Now that they are bounded in by gashes of tarmac, poisoned by insecticides and surrounded by equally hungry badgers, it is little wonder that hedgehogs face a struggle to survive.

It might seem a bitter paradox that the more their populations plummet, so the more we proclaim our love for them. Yet perhaps there is an opportunity here. 'Nature,' as Mark Cocker has put it, 'is slipping from these islands; slowly, steadily, inexorably, field by field, dyke by dyke.' The call to do something seems to most of us too abstract, too divorced from the fauna around us to serve as a summons to action. Who better, then, to serve as the public face of a campaign to restore our wildlife than hedgehogs? A statutory obligation on the government to restore their numbers would work to the good of many other species as well – including invertebrates. The prize for a political party prepared to stand up for Mrs Tiggy-Winkle would be a rich one.

Notes on... Quince Rod Liddle

I recently bought some quinces in our local farmshop as part of my new policy of investing heavily in right-wing fruit, vegetables and legumes. This undertaking, born of principle, has meant a surfeit of cauliflower in our diet, the brassica having been identified by the Democratic party congresswoman Alexandria Ocasio-Cortez as a signifier of white colonialism.

That the quince is decidedly right of centre is surely beyond dispute. It was first grown in England by Edward I, the 'Hammer of the Scots', a man who would have made short work of Nicola Sturgeon. In the 5th century BC the fruit cropped up in Aristophanes's play *The Acharnians*, when the farmer Dicaeopolis remarks to a teenage sex-worker: 'Oh! my gods! what bosoms! Hard as a quince! Come, my treasures, give me voluptuous kisses!' Aristophanes was clearly not a signatory to the #MeToo movement. A couple of centuries later, Callimachus tells us how Acontius uses a quince to pull some chick in the garden of Aphrodite, thus establishing the quince as the go-to symbol for elderly men pursuing underaged women. I don't know if Jimmy Savile ever mentioned quinces.

The fruit resembles a degenerate pear – a pear which has made bad choices in its life. Downy and squat. The tree from which it emerges is a delight, especially in early May when fecund with pink blossom, which is the time that famous perfume begins to emanate. A rich, cloying, decadent aroma reminiscent of Paco Rabanne's 1 Million deodorant, which my wife has banned me from using because she considers the scent 'effeminate'. That perfume stays with you – in the fruit bowl, when you are peeling it and, most of all, while it is being cooked.

Like all good food, and especially right-wing food, the quince requires work, time and an appetite for deferred gratification. It is a bugger to prepare. Peel and core a quince and you will find a swede can be sliced through like butter. The flesh of the quince is fibrously obstinate and the core intractable; be careful with that knife. When you have finished peeling and quartering, set the seeds aside in case a member of the Liberal Democrats comes over. They are rich in cyanide. Toast them and tell him they are pumpkin seeds. That's the best way I can think of to make a lefty turn blue.

Cook those quarters gently. Either poach in a couple of inches of sugared water, a dash of honey and perhaps a strand of thyme in a saucepan on the stove top, or in a bath of the same in the oven. The recipe instructions vary as to how long you should do this – some suggest 40 minutes. Rubbish. You need at least two hours on a low heat. Only then will the quince reveal its magic – the gradual metamorphosis from a wan, pale yellow to a rich crimson, the anthocyanins doing their work. Add another hour or so if you're making quince cheese from the pulp and then another six to rest, before straining and cooking again with added sugar. It will set just fine due to its natural load of pectin.

But I prefer the quartered fruit to still have a little bite; five or six segments and the reserved cooking juice will transform your apple crumble with a gentle tartness. You can purée the red fruit into an accompaniment for duck, or simply serve as they are, with their gloriously red and sticky cooking juice, topped with cream.

Notes on... Historical re-enactments
Christopher Brown

Wimborne Militia of Dorset prides itself on being the only formally commissioned 'private army' in England. We're well known locally but less well known in California, which is perhaps why Facebook once banned our homepage, thinking we were a right-wing Trumpian 'militia'. Its algorithm seemingly did not recognise historical re-enactment societies, which is a shame. They are an important part of British cultural life.

I've been a historical re-enactor since 1983 and I've found that my fellow amateur historians are happy with the moniker of 'mostly harmless' eccentrics. The Wimborne Militia, a band of about 50, receives from the town council a commission 'to further historical research into the history of the town and its surrounds, in particular events pertaining to the 17th century'. As part of our commission, we have planted and maintained a public Physick Garden of plants and herbs for medicinal, culinary and decorative purposes.

At the annual 'mayor making' we escort the outgoing Wimborne mayor to the town hall to ensure the safe return of the solid silver chains of office. The soon to be ex-mayor buys the militia a drink to thank us for our service. After the ceremony, the new mayor is paraded home and invited to buy a drink for the militia to ensure our loyalty for the coming year of office.

When our group was banned from Facebook, we asked the BBC for help as they appeared to have a link to the elusive Facebook offices. Thankfully we were quickly reinstated. Other innocent historical groups in the US have experienced similar expulsion.

Although you can find a re-enactment group for almost any period of history, the English Civil War, disgracefully under-taught in schools, is the most popular. It inspires the most impressive battle recreations, sometimes involving thousands of people, who fight each other with pikes, muskets, cannons and cavalry. At Chalke Valley History Festival we have built an encampment and working examples of devices such as da Vinci's 'Ratchet Cannon' and a handheld 'Eprouvette' for grading and testing gunpowder.

There is, of course, a less serious side to this quest for 'authenticity'. One of my most memorable experiences was in the summer of 1985, when members of the Sealed Knot Society recreated the Duke of Monmouth's rebellion to commemorate the 300th anniversary of the last major armed rebellion in England. We began with Monmouth's landing at Lyme Regis, and followed the route he took to Somerset, complete with skirmishes, before ending with the final defeat at Sedgemoor. Unbeknown to the commanders of the two armies, during the re-enactment of the battle of Midsomer Norton, someone arranged for the police to come on to the battlefield with blue lights and sirens to arrest the protagonists, clap them in irons and cart them off. The villains took it well and even the more historically pedantic participants were able to accept this small revision of events.

Notes on... Passport stamps Sean Thomas

As a travel writer, I can get blasé about many aspects of travel: the free five-handed massage, the private plunge-pool out the back, those odd bits of overchilled orangey cheddar in an average Biz Class lounge.

But one slightly childish thing that always pleases me is stamps in my passport. They should be emotionally meaningless: they are, after all, tiny and potentially annoying examples of frontier bureaucracy, ways and means by which a nation keeps tabs on you.

And yet the other day I was going through the airport at Ibiza and getting my Spanish exit stamp – a Brexit benefit or

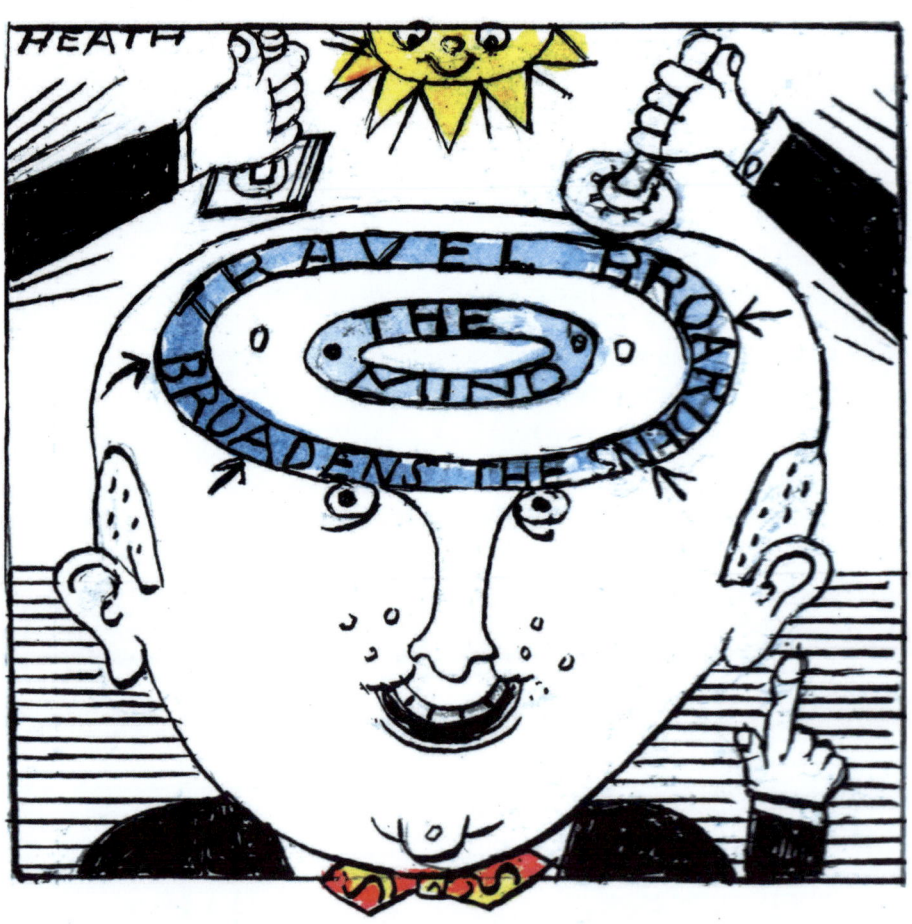

drawback depending on how you feel – and the nice passport lady flicked through my passport, seeking a rare empty page, and said: 'Wow, you have a lot of stamps.' Like a five-year-old, I practically glowed with pride.

Because I do have a lot of stamps. And sometimes I simply like to look at them. I take out my passport and browse these small colourful paper tattoos of red tape, these laughter lines of a travelling lifetime, with as much pleasure as I might look at photos of Bhutan or Belize.

Right now my passport is so full of stamps it is in danger of filling up. However, there is a fair chance that this won't happen – not because I have any intention of ceasing my travels, but because most countries (including and especially those of the EU) are moving on from the archaic era of physical stamps. In future our comings and goings will be monitored digitally – and speedily.

This will, of course, be great for shortening airport queues, and useful for Brits and border police trying to tot up whether they've exceeded their allotted 90 days per 180 in the EU: the computer will say yea or nay, and presumably give warnings.

But it also means we will kiss goodbye to the romance of the exotic stamp, that reminder of the time we crossed from, say, Chile to Bolivia via the Andes and the salt plains, that hour we traversed the emotionally tricky no man's land from Eilat in Israel to Sinai, Egypt. Or that first time we landed in the USA and got one of the simplest stamps of all. The frontier dude smiles as he kerchunks his imprint and says: 'Welcome to America.'

In my decades of travel, I have acquired some seriously – to my mind – exotic and wonderful stamps: Armenia, Madagascar, Greenland, Laos, Ethiopia, Easter Island, Vatican City, Oman. Some of the smallest countries demand entire pages of your passport – looking at you, Cambodia. Others make barely a dent, like France or Thailand, which is useful as I go there a lot.

Then there are the special stamps to truly esoteric destinations. My personal favourite is probably the one I got going into the quasi-independent ecclesiastical republic of Mount Athos in northern Greece. Not only was it fabulously rare, because they only let in a few dozen men (and no women) per week. It was also lavishly beautiful: the double-headed eagle of Byzantium, returned to life and impressed on my passport pages.

It was certainly more cheerful than the stamp I once got from the British embassy in Bangkok, which paid to have me repatriated from Thailand after I really mis-behaved. That stamp said 'Impound Passport on Arrival in London'. And so they did.

Yet I miss that stamp too.

Notes on... Lobsters Margaret Mitchell

The night before I moved a pet lobster into my flat, I ate a*gnolotti all' aragosta* for dinner. It was possible that my soon-to-be companion, Snips McGee – who I inherited from a friend – would outlive me (the oldest lobster on record was estimated to be 140 years old) and I wanted one last plate of lobster ravioli, hold the moral hang-ups.

The French author Gérard de Nerval also owned a pet lobster, which he took for walks on a blue silk leash. 'They are peaceful, serious creatures,' he said. 'They know the secrets of the sea, they don't bark, and they don't gnaw upon one's monadic privacy like dogs do.' How I wish that were true. My Snips didn't bark, but it was hard to find monadic or any other kind of privacy with an infant-sized cockroach by my bed.

Salvador Dali associated lobsters with the bedroom. His lobster-shaped 'Aphrodisiac Telephone' was designed to look erotic. In 'The Dream of Venus', naked female models are covered with lobsters. He collaborated with Elsa Schiaparelli on the 'lobster dress', which was included in Wallis Simpson's wedding trousseau and worn shortly before her marriage to Edward VIII. Why did he consider lobsters erotic? I shared a bedroom with a lobster and just don't get it. But such sensuality captivated the Dutch still life painters long before Dali. You'll find many a ripe red lobster banqueting with skulls and pocket watches in a de Heem or de Ring in the Wallace Collection.

Despite what the TV show *Friends* might tell you, lobsters don't mate for life. Female lobsters wield their pheromones feverishly and with little subtlety. She wafts her urine into the alpha male lobster's domain, seducing him and mating with him for about two weeks before letting the next lady in the line-up repeat the process. What's more, lobsters excrete from their faces into the faces of their opponents and mates, sending chemically encoded hate mail or love letters.

It's difficult to see past lobsters' hard exteriors, but that doesn't mean they don't have feelings. 'We need to look for ways to move beyond our own emotional responses to these animals and instead look at the evidence about what is actually going on in them,' says Dr Jonathan Birch, a professor at LSE and principal investigator on the Foundations of Animal Sentience project. The project has discovered that several decapod crustaceans, including lobsters, might be sentient based on specific behavioural and neurological criteria. I wonder if this means they could be capable of love, or something like it.

Like star-crossed lovers, Snips and I were of separate worlds. His blue blood belonged in open waters, not a 60-litre tank in my student flat. Out of boredom, misery or perhaps indifference, he crushed his oxygen filter and eventually suffocated. I was grief-stricken – not only because it was more

than a century too soon, but because I had loved him. I buried him at sea.

    Months later, I indulged in a lobster roll on a trip to the coast. The sun was out, children were playing and I was happy. I considered the conclusion that Dali and de Heem had drawn before: all that's left to do with the facts of mortality is to savour them.

Notes on... Going grey Cosmo Landesman

In the wake of recent research by New York University's Grossman School of Medicine, scientists think a treatment for stopping our hair going grey – and even reversing it – may soon be possible. Their optimism is based on early positive experiments with mice, which is great news if you're a mouse, but what if you're a man over 60 and totally grey like me?

Yes, women go grey too – but it's different for them. The ones I know don't make a big existential drama out of it the way men like me do. Women simply dye their hair or just let it go grey. Men panic and turn to desperate measures like concealing highlights, expensive anti-grey shampoos, exotic toners and total dye jobs.

And usually with tragic results. Having a dye job is the male equivalent of having a boob job – it looks odd. Getting rid of grey is sold to men as a way of getting back the younger you but you end up just looking older because your young hair draws attention to your older face.

Why do men do it? Partly vanity and partly virility. To the male mind, the loss of hair colour signals to women a loss of youth, which signals a loss of virility, which signals you're probably bad in bed – at least that's the irrational male fear.

But women tend to be kind about men who are going grey. When my hair first started changing colour in my thirties, female friends insisted I had nothing to worry about; my grey hair, they claimed, made me look 'distinguished'. Instead of thanking them for this vote of confidence, I would complain: 'But I don't want to look bloody distinguished! I want to look sexy and shaggable!'

As time passed and my hair got greyer and greyer, female friends kept reminding me that ageing was a fact of life and I might as well just relax. These were excellent words of wisdom but I ignored them and began to dye my hair. First a trendy hair stylist I knew coloured it an orangey red. I looked like Tintin's granddad. Then I tried dying it black. I imagined I'd look like a cool Nick Cave – but I ended up like an over-dyed Elvis.

By the end of my fifties I had gone from 'distinguished' to 'silver fox'. When a date first called me that I didn't understand the term. For starters, there's nothing silver about my hair. It's grey. Battleship grey. A rainy afternoon by the English seaside grey. As for the fox bit, there's nothing foxy – clever, cunning, fast of foot – about me. I'm more silver sloth than silver fox. Later, I was relieved to learn it was meant as a compliment – as in a good-looking older man.

I wonder if this new promise of a grey-free future has arrived a little too late, at least for us old grey guys. Society isn't as youth-obsessed as it was. We no longer envy the young; we pity them.

Increasingly, dyeing your hair is seen as something naff. That's why so many celebrities have stopped doing it. Paul McCartney – at 76 – stopped dyeing, and so did Richard Gere, Sylvester Stallone and even Melvyn Bragg. Brad Pitt is so cool that he added grey to his hair. Nowadays, the older men I talk to don't want to look like their younger selves – they want to look like glad-to-be-grey George Clooney. And so do I.

Notes on... Halloween turnips
Melanie McDonagh

You see them everywhere in vast orange mounds: pumpkins, piles of pumpkins, large enough to be turned into a coach in Whole Foods, a bargain 65p in M&S. Halloween, in terms of retail, means orange for pumpkin and black for witches. Round our way, a pumpkin outside the front door means that the household is receptive to tots and teenagers coming round in costume looking for sweets.

Pah! When I was small in Ireland, there was none of this pumpkin lark. We never saw pumpkins, except in *Cinderella*, where it was the exotic element of the story. Pumpkins are a visible symbol of what happened to All Hallows' Eve, when the celebrations for the feast of ghosts and divination were taken to America with Irish emigrants… and then somehow came back again. And when Halloween returned from the New World, it was changed hideously. A night for ghost stories and simple games turned into a gore fest; the nuts and apples (and loose change) children collected in their scary costume from the neighbours turned into chocolates; and the humble turnip was replaced by a pumpkin.

Come again? A turnip? Yep, a turnip. Or properly, a swede turnip. These excellent root vegetables, popular in Ireland boiled, mashed and served with pepper, were sometimes hollowed out, carved with holes for a face and used as lanterns for lights or candles. The effect was charming. They're much harder than pumpkins to carve, being solid all the way through, but the residue can be served up for dinner and is nice eaten raw, sweet in flavour. The turnip is obviously not one of those pre-Christian relics of the festivities themselves, having been introduced in the 19th century, but it's still more solidly traditional than the American import.

In fact, the brilliant social historian Ronald Hutton in *The Stations of the Sun* observes that illuminated turnips were found in England too, chiefly in Somerset, 'known as "spunkies" or "punkies"… being the common Somerset name for ignited marsh gas… The carved faces, outlined by the candle within, were taken in that district as warnings of death, and used to scare unpopular people'. A less plausible theory was that they represented the souls of unbaptised babies.

So, here's my proposal. Let's eschew the too-big, too-garish American pumpkin and replace it with the Irish/Scottish turnip. There is no way a turnip will rival a pumpkin in size, but do you really need something as big as a cauldron? If I could be bothered, I could probably make a case for the turnip being kinder to the planet, on the basis that it takes less water and less space to grow and is more likely to be eaten afterwards.

Actually, let's get back to basics generally with Halloween. Let's eschew the

chocolate treats for that characteristic Halloween edible: barm brack, a yeasted fruit bread which you serve with butter and which has a ring inside – the finder will be the first to marry. Or colcannon: mashed potato mixed with cabbage or kale, which might hide a coin (for wealth) or a ring (for marriage).

Boo to pumpkins and all they stand for. Bring back proper Halloween.

Notes on... Orcas Simon Barnes

Male killer whales are all mummy's boys. That's not a revelation; their curious and intense social lives have been studied for decades, but the extent to which a male orca depends on his mother has been revealed by new research, which shows that mothers routinely sacrifice their food and their energies for their enormous male offspring, compromising their own health and their ability to produce more young.

Orcas or killer whales – the former name is used more often these days – are not whales but big dolphins, up to eight metres long. They're fierce enough under any name, but curiously selective in their ferocity. And that's all about culture.

Not ours: theirs. The cultural life of orcas is a subject of scientific debate, and its implications are extensive. The idea that only humans have culture – that culture defines the separation of humanity from everything else that lives – is long exploded and orcas have helped greatly with the exploding.

The orcas of the Northwest Pacific are divided into three distinct populations, and the differences between them are not physiological but cultural. The differences show in how and what they hunt. There are

the offshores, who specialise in deep-sea fish; there are the residents, who prefer salmon; and there are the transients, who specialise in marine mammals – seals and whales, up to and including the blue whale.

These different populations are called ecotypes and they don't mix. (There are perhaps five different ecotypes in the Antarctic.) All orcas have the equipment to feed on each other's preferred food, but they don't even try. They stick to their own tastes and their own kind. They are very picky about it – captive animals of one ecotype refuse unfamiliar food to the point of starvation.

They are also xenophobic. They live in very tight matrilinear groups and, most unusually, all the young stay with the maternal group for the rest of their lives. Females become relatively independent of their mothers and meet their own feeding needs, but males don't. Individuals leave the group for short periods to mate outside their group.

Orcas are deeply loyal to others of the same group and they go to considerable lengths to avoid groups of a different ecotype. Each group upholds both its separateness and its identity with its own range of distinct sounds. This sense of community and shared purpose helps them to operate as brilliantly effective co-operative hunters.

Orcas are gaudy animals. Sharks are just as fast and just as well armed, and they are coloured in ways that keep them relatively hidden even in open water, but orcas, with their dramatic black and white patterns, stand out at distance. It's been speculated that it's like football: they gain more from being able to keep tabs on their colleagues – teammates – than they would from being hidden.

This is a species that makes us ask troubling questions, not about orcas but about humanity. The self-sacrificing mother is one such question; their cultural life is another and bigger one. Orcas are more remarkable than people ever thought when writing them off as mere killers: but why should we be surprised? All we have to do is read Darwin: 'The difference in mind between man and the higher animals, great as it is, certainly is one of degree and not of kind.'

Notes on... Bengal cats Miranda Morrison

Over the past year and a half, I have been victimised by my neighbour's cat. Bollinger the Bengal weighs just seven pounds and has a silly dangly bell around his neck, but he manages to terrorise both me and my two cats. He fights my male cat, George, so viciously that I fear he might kill him.

Nothing irks me more than watching people cooing around Bollinger when they see his ocelot-like frame. While some Bengal cats can be wonderful pets, their wild instincts make them territorial and aggressive, as well as horribly effective hunters that can ravage bird populations.

In the summer of 2022, the town of Walldorf in southwest Germany introduced a cat curfew to protect the breeding season of the endangered crested lark. Pet owners in breach of the curfew risked being fined between €500 and €50,000.

In the US, Bengal cats are banned in four states, including Seattle and New York, and there are restrictions in six others. Most states demand a permit or that cats are several generations removed from the Asian leopard breed. No such legislation exists in the UK, although there have been calls for owners to require a licence under the 1976 Dangerous Wild Animals Act. Bollinger often stalks me down the road, growling and hissing. He seems to spend half his time in my garden or on my windowsills. He torments my cats through the glass. He knocks over flowerpots and leaves scratch marks on the panes. I now close my curtains when I go out. The flat looks more like a nuclear bunker than a relaxing home.

Other cats in the area are regularly attacked and their owners are permanently stressed. One neighbour has kept his cat inside for more than a year. Plenty of people have had to chase Bollinger out of their flats and into the street to break up fights. Before he came along, life was more harmonious. The odd cat fight settled any disputes. Now I have a modest collection of weapons to deter him: a high-pressure water pistol, a bag of potatoes and a washing-up bottle filled with sugary water.

Cats have a right to roam in British law, unlike dogs and livestock. Extreme nuisance can, however, lead to local councils issuing antisocial behaviour orders. A few years ago, a group of cat owners in Roehampton proved that a local Bengal was wreaking havoc by going into people's houses and savaging their pets. The Asbo meant its owner had to keep the cat inside. If they didn't comply, they'd be committing a criminal offence.

Bollinger wants to roam and hunt, which is fair enough – but perhaps Pimlico is the wrong terrain for him. My mother's cat, Hector, is a quarter Bengal but is lovely to both cats and humans. He is, however, known as the Robin Hood of Putney, because he likes to slaughter squirrels, who otherwise would be ransacking birds' nests and stripping bark off trees. My aunt, on the other hand, has a pair of Bengals who seem quite miserable. They aren't allowed out and instead exert all their wild energy on torturing the dog, a Rhodesian Ridgeback bred for hunting bears and lions. It's all rather sad.

Notes on... Italians Nicholas Farrell

For a few years before coming to Italy, I lived in Paris and I cannot tell you the life-enhancing difference I felt as I crossed the frontier from France into Italy in my metallic burgundy Honda Prelude.

On arrival at the Italian motorway toll that stifling summer of 1998, I discovered I had no money and that the sun had melted my bank card which I had left on the dashboard. The charming young woman on the tollgate simply gave me a form to fill in and waved me through with a smile. Isn't this how we should run the world?

I remember once being stopped by two Italian police patrol cars in the dead of night when well over the limit. Instead of them breathalysing me, we started to have a discussion about the Mussolini biography I had written. 'Mussolini was a very misunderstood man,' I assured the Italian police. 'Hitler gave him such a bad press.' '*Molto bravo*, Farrell. Just write the truth about Il Duce, OK?' the *maresciallo* said as he sent me on my way.

The French, on the other hand, take a sadistic pleasure in denying people a conversation, let alone a solution. I remember Paris only for the cold indifference of Parisians to others, and their inability to smile.

In preferring the Italians to the French I am not alone. The great French novelist Stendhal detested his fellow countrymen but adored Italians, and spent much of his adult life in Italy trying to explain why. With the exception of Napoleon, in whose army he had served and whom he idolised, Stendhal felt that his fellow countrymen were bigoted, frigid, artificial, insincere, arrogant, money-grubbing, cynical and vulgar.

The French 'never sin out of love or hate', he wrote, but only for personal gain. The Italians are frank, natural and uninhibited, and thus sincerely passionate – as are their sins. Whereas the French had bridled passion long ago, the Italians remained ruled by it, even to the point of madness.

I have been in Italy now for 20 years and have six small children whose mother is Italian. If I had not been barred from voting in the UK's Brexit referendum by the 15 years abroad rule, I would unquestionably have voted Leave because I love Europe but detest the EU. I have no wish to become an Italian. I do not feel Italian, never will. But nor do I feel European.

I am an exile, not in France, thank God – but in Italy. Obviously, I prefer the Italians to the tunnel-vision Germans and increasingly, too, even to the smug British. But above all, I prefer them to the French.

The Italians are just far less uptight, arrogant, condescending and negative. And they are far more fun. Yes, Italy is a byword for dishonesty and deceit, and after two decades here I know all about how that pans out.

But incredible as it may seem, I would trust an Italian more than I would a Frenchman. I would go further. I would rather be in a first world war trench with an Italian than a Frenchman as we go over the top.

The French may be technically and rationally right on everything under the sun. But the Italians are emotionally right, which is priceless. That is why they smile at strangers; and it is that smile that gave us the Renaissance.

Notes on... Cruise ship pianists Tom Yarwood

When Crystal Cruises invited me to join their flagship as the guest classical pianist for a springtime voyage around the Aegean, I had my doubts. Inspecting their website, I anticipated jazz-age glamour, Art Deco-inflected design and gourmet cuisine. But playing Beethoven on a boat? What about the noise, and the movement – not to mention the psychological effect of the environment on my interpretation? How, for instance, would my inner Richter fare in a face-off with my inner Liberace in a venue called the Galaxy Lounge?

I have a genetic piano-seeking compulsion, however. I play them wherever I can find them. Could a luxury passenger vessel, I asked myself, really be much worse than a rowdy London pub? A Brazilian jungle lodge? Besides, perhaps great music strikes one more powerfully when heard in unusual circumstances.

As I climb aboard in Athens, I muse that the cruise-ship ivory-tickler in his crisply pressed tailcoat is an elegant remnant from a vanished age, when travel was always sociable and slow. I half expect Bertie Wooster to bustle past me, whistling a jaunty tune, or Hercule Poirot to appear at the top of the gangplank. I will be treated as a guest on the ship, I've been told. And as I have only three concerts to give in a fortnight, vast vistas of leisure open up before me.

My recitals are designed to complement our itinerary – a lovely tour of the Greek islands during Holy Week. One recital is about the sea, with plenty of shimmering Ravel; the next about myths and legends, with my own piano reductions of Liszt and Beethoven; and the third about Easter, with works by Haydn and Bach.

I catch a dance performance in which a lithe young couple high-kick their way through a number of soft-rock tracks with exemplary skill, and wearing little besides a few carefully placed viridian streamers. The audience is large and demonstrative. I become lugubrious. No way will my own shows measure up to this. Should I find colourful lighting? A nubile dancer to gyrate around the Steinway?

As it turns out, I needn't have worried. It's no joke trying to execute the dazzling passagework in Debussy's 'Reflets dans l'eau' when one is actually *sur l'eau*, and said *l'eau* is vigorously animated by squalls from the Sahara. But the music comes across fine for the most part, and my audience, though relatively small, is knowledgeable – including a few accomplished amateur pianists and a professional piano tuner.

Indeed, it is my warm relationship with fellow guests that proves the unexpected boon of cruising. I can scarcely leave my 'stateroom' without bumping into people keen to talk about music. And bound up with music is emotion: I hear of childhood, business, marriage, despair, revenge. There are invitations to dinner and tea-time confabs about the creative careers of children and grandchildren. It's like performing at a summer camp, but with better food and ever-changing views.

Gazing out at the black sea cliffs as we sail into the flooded caldera of Santorini at dawn, or digesting my daily dose of profiteroles as I wander along the sparkling shore of carefree, car-free little Hydra, life feels grand. I begin to wonder if I need face the awful solitude of a landlubbers' concert hall again.

Notes on... Smoked salmon Henry Jeffreys

I'm just about old enough to remember when smoked salmon was a rare treat. Then, around 1986 or 1987, suddenly it was everywhere. There were smoked salmon sandwiches at M&S, it was stuffed into lurid-looking canapés with cream cheese, and Christmas became a riot of salty fish. For me, smoked salmon is as emblematic of the 1980s as red Porsches, huge mobile phones and the Pet Shop Boys. But it's almost always a disappointment, that acrid taste only palatable with lots of lemon juice and butter. I'd much rather have potted shrimp.

It's a far cry from how Scottish smoked salmon is supposed to be. It was first produced, not in Scotland but in London by Jewish immigrants in the late 19th century. They took the Eastern European way of smoking fish and applied it to Scottish salmon from Billingsgate Market. It became a highly prized delicacy and there were dozens of smokehouses in the East End, but in the 1980s industrialised smoked salmon killed them all, except for one, H. Forman & Son.

'We survived by luck more than strategy. We just didn't change,' said Lance Forman,

great-grandson of the founder. The business has suffered flood, fire and the attentions of the London Development Agency, which appropriated its land for the Olympics. But it now has a new factory and restaurant located, appropriately enough, in an area of Bow known as Fish Island. London Cure smoked salmon is now a protected food such as Stilton cheese or Iberico ham. To qualify, it has to be Scottish salmon cured using only salt and oak smoke in Hackney, Tower Hamlets or Newham. In this traditional technique, only the outside of the fish comes into contact with smoke. This is then cut off, so the salmon underneath is dried and concentrated, but doesn't taste of smoke.

In the industrial process the fish probably comes from Norway (it is 20 per cent cheaper). It needs only to be smoked in Scotland to be called Scottish smoked salmon. It may be brined rather than salted to preserve moisture. It might be sprayed with liquid smoke rather than properly smoked, and sugar may be added to balance the saltiness required for a long shelf life. Hence that acrid taste.

For many years, Forman was the only one smoking salmon in London, but now there is a young pretender; a Scotsman, appropriately enough. Max Bergius, who has started the Secret Smokehouse near London Fields, began smoking in his back garden in Stepney. The locals noticed it was something more interesting than Benson & Hedges and took an interest. 'My fish reminded them of the old days when east London was full of smokehouses,' says Max.

Both companies use very fresh farmed salmon. 'We buy fish that was swimming two days ago – it still has rigor mortis,' Lance Forman told me. They offer different cuts, lean or fatty, depending on your taste. I preferred the fatty cut. 'That's your Jewish heritage!' he told me. Forman also makes a wildly expensive smoked wild salmon, which tastes like a totally different species.

Both claim not have tried their rival's fish, which I don't believe for a moment. They taste very different: the Forman product is like concentrated fresh salmon, whereas the Secret Smokehouse stuff has a creamy, oaky note, like a white Burgundy. Both cost about twice the price of normal smoked salmon. Not expensive for such good fish, but far too good for an M&S sarnie.

Notes on... Tarot reading Daisy Waugh

It's 8.57 on a Friday evening in the spring of 2016 and I'm at home, waiting for an obscure American radio talk show to come online. For the next hour I'll be answering listeners' love queries with the aid of my Tarot-reading skills, and out of respect to all the lovesick Americans out there I've made a real effort to stay sober. Which is quite an achievement because, downstairs, my friends are slugging it out over the EU referendum. Nobody understands what they're talking about, as usual, but I'm feeling left out. So I lay three cards on the table and ask the Tarot: 'Who's going to win?' Do read on…

The radio show's a one-off. Normally, I sit in a darkened booth somewhere in Chelsea and wait for punters to walk in off the street. They cross my palm with silver – *and oh, the things I've heard…* which I obviously can't reveal. Enough of this! America is calling, and I have advice to dispense. It's a bad line. I can't work out who's saying what to whom, or whether we're even on air. The producers are in Seattle; the two hosts are in California. And I am here in Barnes, SW13, with the future of our nation laid out on my tabletop. All of which makes it hard to concentrate.

Worse, nobody's phoning in. The Californian hosts drum up a flirtatious squabble to kill time, involving… storage space? An orange case, perhaps? One of them makes a joke about 'DOG' being 'GOD' spelled backwards, and for a moment, from Seattle to LA, panic reigns. We all agree that we *all love DOGS*. And then – thank dog – there's a caller. Denise? Denis? I can't hear what s/he is saying, but s/he wants to know… something about love, I presume. You'd be amazed at the things I can learn from the cards when everything's going right. Tonight, though, I feel a fraud, more concerned with my referendum findings than with Denis's lonely nights.

'Great news, Denis,' I say. 'I think you're going to be very happy.' Denis has to leave after that. Then it's just us again, filling space. 'We're asking listeners out there to tell us what little things make them happy,' says one of my hosts for the seventh time. 'What little things make you happy, Daisy?' 'Raindrops on roses and whiskers on kittens,' I reply. 'And dogs, obviously.' 'Oops, wait up, Daisy! Sorry to interrupt. We have Andrea on the line. Andrea in Wisconsin! Welcome to the show! What little things make you happy, Andrea?'

There is an incredibly long silence. And then: 'WHAT! ME?' It would be impossible to exaggerate the rage that is packed into those two short syllables. We have a nutjob. They cut her off. And finally the show is over, and I'm all alone with my referendum results. Will it be in or out? Book in for a reading, my pretties, and I'll tell you. Forty quid for 30 minutes. I may even throw in some advice on your love life for free… because we all need that.

Notes on... Swiss Army knives
Andrew Watts

Victorinox, makers of the Swiss Army knife (all other manufacturers must refer to their products as 'Swiss-style knives'), recently announced that the company is working to develop a knife without any blades in anticipation of modern legislation and safety-conscious consumers. A cutting-edge Swiss Army knife will no longer have a cutting edge.

I'm glad this proposal didn't come out before Christmas 2023, the year my wife finally agreed our son could have a knife of his own. She has friends who won't let their children wash up knives in case they injure themselves, but let them watch YouTube unsupervised. My son and I were firmly of the view that all small boys should have a Swiss Army knife – as advised in paragraph one of *The Dangerous Book for Boys*, where it tops the list of 'Essential Kit', above even a really good marble or a pencil and paper to write down the car numbers of criminals. Apart from the Swiss flag, which is a big plus, you never knew when you might need to loosen a screw or open a wine bottle. The only thing he has yet to find a single purpose

for is the 'multipurpose hook' on the back – most guides to the knife suggest it can be used to carry packages tied up with string, but they're not one of his favourite things. He is saving the fish-scaling tool until Halloween, as he's heard that it's perfect for carving pumpkins.

The Swiss Army has always been confident of victory – when the Kaiser asked what its 250,000 soldiers could do if Germany invaded with an army of half a million, a member of the militia replied, 'Shoot twice, then go home' – but including a corkscrew in their standard kit always seemed slightly cocky. In fact, this was only part of the officers' version, the Schweizer Offiziersmesser invented by Carl Elsener's great-grandfather, which the GIs buying them as souvenirs for the folks back home couldn't pronounce and renamed the Swiss Army knife.

Billy Connolly may have always wanted to visit Switzerland, just to see what the army does with those wee red knives, but the original version did actually serve a military purpose. The service rifle used at the time, the Schmidt-Rubin, had screws that needed to be undone to strip and oil them, and soldiers' rations came in cans. The original army issue pocket-knife had a screwdriver, can opener and reamer, with grips made from oak – and a blade.

The fact that the blade folds makes it practically useless as a weapon: if you tried to stab anyone with it, you'd do more damage to yourself than your opponent when it snapped shut on your fingers. According to American survivalist websites – which, possibly due to the influence of the TV series *MacGyver* (where it was the hero's tool of choice), devote a lot of discussion to what they call 'SAKs' – the only way to use them in self-defence is by deploying the awl as a makeshift knuckleduster.

Recruits to the Swiss Army still receive a Swiss Army knife after basic training – but, after previous models failed health and safety, a new version was designed in 2008. It's as much a rite of passage for them as it is for proper small boys in Britain.

Notes on... Rollies Ruari Clark

I recently estimated that, in my smoking life so far and at the age of 29, I have rolled 87,600 cigarettes. The calculation went as follows. Roughly 30 a day for the past six years, maybe 15 a day for four years before that. I attempted to make a reduction for eight months I spent in China, where the most beautiful straights could be bought for the equivalent of 40p per pack. But my mathematical faculties are almost as weak as my pulmonary ones, so I decided to balance those Chinese cigarettes with the thousands of rollies I've been asked to construct for friends, acquaintances and strangers.

Apart from that brief and illicit fling with Chinese yen, I've been a roll-up man from the start. In fact, my relationship with tobacco has proven by far my most enduring and life-enhancing (with apologies and thanks to Milly, Mary, Molly and Mandy). It's a partnership that has given far more than it has taken, and I'd like to put on record my gratitude to that great man Sir Walter Raleigh.

What does my smoking life consist of? If I was to provide a list: 30 small achievements every day (how many can say that?); an act of defiance in the face of life's absurdity; a sense of calm – what David Hockney calls a rest from life. It's also a way of illustrating my cosmopolitanism – did I tell you I can ask for a cigarette in at least four languages (six after a few drinks)? I have a bad cough, too, but we all have our crosses to bear.

I often wonder if the perfect roll-up exists. I know what it looks like. The filter is aligned with the bottom end of the paper, the tobacco is evenly weighted, none protrudes in an unsightly growth, and the two halves of the paper meet in a line as straight as one drawn by Michelangelo. It's this last bit that seems impossible. As hard as I try, the paper is always slightly off. I'm an unintentional Impressionist, when really, I yearn to be a Cubist, all sharp lines and clear edges.

I've only ever had one truly upsetting experience with a hand-rolled cigarette. I used to work on a Devon dairy farm. One summer, I'd spent all day in the fields turning hay. I had pocketed every fag butt, one for each field, smoked as I turned the last row of mown grass. When I finished, the sun falling over Exmoor, I realised I'd run out of tobacco. I unpicked each of my fag ends, delicately removing the unsmoked flakes and constructing a cigarette so lovingly that even Rishi Sunak and Keir Starmer would have been moved to tears by the strength of my devotion. At the final moment, just as I began to turn the paper, a gust of wind blew all my efforts to nought. I think Kipling may well have had a similar experience. What else could produce the line: 'Watch the things you gave your life to, broken,/ And stoop and build 'em up with worn-out tools.'

I'm still trying to roll the perfect cigarette. In the time I've written this

ROLL UP, ROLL UP!

inconsequential piece, I've made six attempts. I got close once, but my thumb slipped at the critical moment. In moments of despair, I question whether I'll ever do it. But I try not to doubt myself too much. I know it will happen one day. As I sit here, I see the smoke curling upwards. Perhaps I should roll another, try again to 'fill the unforgiving minute', make another effort to reach the stars, create perfection and know it when I see it. It's time for attempt number 87,601.

Notes on... Shrove Tuesday Francis Young

In some countries Shrove Tuesday (the day of merrymaking before the rigours of Lent) developed into a 'carnival' that lasted several days, but in England it was only ever a half-day holiday, since it was not an official Church feast day. Apprentices and schoolchildren claimed the right to an afternoon of 'sport', and from at least the 15th century the most popular Shrove Tuesday recreation was 'throwing at cocks'. This was a cruel custom that involved immobilising a cockerel, either by tying its foot to a stake or half burying it in the ground, while bystanders took turns throwing stones, tools and bricks at the cockerel in an attempt to kill it.

The successful killer received the dead bird as a prize, which might account for the custom, since Shrove Tuesday was traditionally the last day before Easter when flesh could be consumed. Sometimes referred to as 'cock threshing' or 'holling at cocks', the custom varied throughout the country, but invariably ended with the fowl's demise.

This throwing at cocks was just one of many English blood sports in an era of casual cruelty to animals but it stands apart from others, such as bear-baiting, cockfighting and dogfighting, because it was the first to attract moral objections. As early as the 1730s letters appeared in newspapers deploring the custom, not so much on the grounds of

its intrinsic cruelty but for its lack of sportsmanship. After all, the tethered or buried cockerel had no chance to defend itself, and the contest was not one of equals like a cockfight.

Killing and maiming animals when they had no chance to escape offended many people precisely because it was not sport in the way they understood it, but rather mindless violence. The 18th century was hardly an era known for its sympathetic treatment of animals, but by the end of the century magistrates in most areas had outlawed throwing at cocks, even though it was often simply replaced by the scarcely more humane alternative of cockfighting.

By the time the last known instance of throwing at cocks took place at Quainton, Buckinghamshire in 1844, it seemed like a barbaric relic of another world. The RSPCA had been founded in 1824, and already campaigns were under way against cockfighting and dogfighting, as well as the inhumane treatment of horses. The early activists for animal welfare were as much concerned with the deleterious moral effects of casual cruelty on human perpetrators as the fate of the animals themselves. The original objections to throwing at cocks emerged from anxieties about public order and gentility; people with refined manners did not want to run into displays of atavistic brutality.

These were the same concerns that brought an end to public hangings in the mid-Victorian period: public enjoyment of the violent deaths of felons was no longer considered acceptable in a 'civilised' nation, even though no mercy was shown towards felons when their executions were hidden from view. The advent of animal welfare was similarly contradictory, and proponents of reform had few concerns about animal sentience or pain.

Nevertheless, change must start somewhere and we have public disgust at a Shrove Tuesday custom to thank for the earliest beginnings of animal welfare.

Notes on... Beef dripping   Angus Colwell

For several years, a debate has raged (mainly on Twitter, now X) over whether animal fats are actually better for you than industrially processed 'seed oils'. The debate became more mainstream thanks to the efforts of the US Health Secretary, Robert F. Kennedy Jnr, whose strategy to Make America Healthy Again involved a back-to-the-land style embrace of animal fats, particularly beef dripping.

The anti-seed oil community use technical-sounding terms like 'linoleic acids' to firm up their side of the debate but fundamentally their point is that our bodies have evolved to process animal fats rather than overly processed stuff. J.D. Vance doesn't cook with seed oils, and RFK congratulated the US chain Steak 'n Shake for switching the frying oil for its chips to beef tallow.

You don't hear all that much here about beef dripping (as tallow is known) unless you happen to be in Newcastle or Yorkshire. It fell out of fashion for a few reasons: industrial seed oils were cheaper, more people became vegetarian, and BSE didn't help beef fat's reputation either. We also started to kid ourselves that we could make deep-fried foods somehow 'healthier' if the oil contained fewer calories.

RFK's endorsement of dripping threatens to make the issue partisan. Are you a beef-fat boy or a seed-oil boy? But let's put politics aside and focus on the most important matter when it comes to food – taste. The vital point is that food fried in beef dripping tastes better.

I visited Marlow Fish Bar in south London for research, which is one of a handful of London chippies that still uses dripping. The whole shop is filled with the amazing honk of beef fat, and I was delighted to discover that it serves one of the best fish and chips I've had. Was the taste of beef dripping making me more virile, more manly? I like to think so. My one note of caution is to ensure that chips fried in dripping are eaten quickly, otherwise they go soggy.

Chef Ed McIlroy is well aware of the superiority of dripping, and he is helping to lead the comeback. At Tollington's, a chippy in Finsbury Park that he has converted into a tapas bar, they serve 'chips bravas' which are cooked in dripping. Ed buys 40kg of aged beef fat from the butcher every couple of weeks, then renders the fat down into a liquid. The chips are given their third fry in the beef fat. 'It's so much better for you than a lot of oils that are available on the market,' he says. 'That's evident when we clean out the machines. The side that we have [other] oils in are often caked in carbon deposits and solidified fat, whereas when we empty the beef fat side of the fryer, the metal is untarnished and relatively clean.'

Cooking with seed oil is a sad attempt to fiddle at the margins, to console yourself that because you're frying in sunflower oil your dinner is slightly less atherosclerotic.

But there's a better way. Fry less, but fry better – in lard, or beef dripping, or duck fat, or something similar. Whether beef dripping really is better for your health is, as they say, 'outside the scope' of a 'Notes on…' column. But come on. You want it to be. I want it to be. If not for our arteries, then for our souls.

Notes on... Ninjas Francis Pike

One of my favourite scenes in *Kill Bill*, Quentin Tarantino's black comedy martial arts film, is the meeting of Beatrix 'the Bride' Kiddo, played by Uma Thurman, with sword-maker Hattori Hanzo at his scruffy sushi bar in Okinawa.

Hanzo: What do you want with Hattori Hanzo?
Kiddo: I need Japanese steel.
Hanzo: Why do you need Japanese steel?
Kiddo: I have vermin to kill.
Hanzo: You must have big rats, to need Hattori Hanzo's steel.

Tarantino filched his sword-maker's name from history. Hattori Hanzo was a real ninja (or rather, the historically correct word *shinobi*). Born in 1542, he spent his life in the service of the shogun Tokugawa Ieyasu and compiled the manual *Shinobi Hiden* (*Legends of Ninja Secrets*).

Japan's most famous swordsman was Miyamoto Musashi (c.1584–1645), a *kensei* – sword saint – who, in a record 62 undefeated duels, became renowned for his double-bladed style. This involved using a full-length katana sword in combination with a short (less than 2ft), slightly curved *wakizashi* sword.

It is an inauthentic straight-bladed version of this weapon (not a genuine ninja sword) that has been banned in Britain under 'Ronan's law', named after the young man stabbed to death with a sword purchased online.

By contrast, in 1960 the leader of the Japanese Socialist party, Inejiro Asanuma, was murdered on stage with a genuine *wakizashi*. A decade later the great novelist Yukio Mishima used a *wakizashi* blade to commit ritual suicide in an act of lamentation for Japan's loss of its samurai spirit.

Japan did not need Hollywood to create the ninja mythology. It could do that by itself. The word 'ninja' itself is less than 100 years old. In the 1930s, the ninja movie genre *jidaigeki* (literally 'period drama'), Japan's equivalent of the western, took off. Not surprisingly, it coincided with the rise of the samurai *bushido* (code of honour) cult in bastardised form which underlay the rise of ultranationalism.

The emphasis of *jidaigeki* films is highly choreographed swordplay, the equivalent of gunfights in westerns. But neither this, nor the common image of creeping around castles at night, represents the real art of the ninja. As the medieval historian Professor Yuji Yamada of Mie University has noted, the ninja should 'make no sound, leave no smell and get no fame or honour even if you have accomplished the extraordinary'.

Mie prefecture, and particularly Iga Ueno castle, about 50 miles southeast of Kyoto, lies at the heart of the ninja legend. The most famous ninja school, Iga-ryu, developed here. Training included climbing, the use of scaling hooks, lock-picking and the dark arts of poisons and explosives. Concealment, disguise, diplomacy and spying were complimentary skills.

Fittingly, Mie is the home of the last ninja. Jinichi Kawakami, the 21st head of the Iga-ryu, is now an old man and does not intend to name a successor. The time of the ninja has passed. Kawakami, his snaggle-tooth grin apart, looks as harmless as your typical Japanese salaryman: a perfect disguise for a modern-day ninja.

Notes on... Indexes Dennis Duncan

We all know a sleb memoir is rarely the work of the celebrity, but the ghostwriter is not the only anonymous voice at work – an indexer can play a quietly subversive part too. One of my favourite index moments is in Shaun Ryder's autobiography (*Twisting My Melon* – of course!), towards the end of the S's: 'sinus problems, 2; splitting up with Denise, 63; splitting up with Felicia, 320; splitting up with Oriole, 295; splitting up with Trish, 246–7; sunburnt in Valencia, 141–2; teeth, 327–8; thyroid problem, 320, 326; UFOs seen, 33–4.'

Teeth, UFOs, hypochondria, and failed relationships on a doomed, never-learn loop. Of course, it is part of the nature of an index – the arbitrariness of alphabetical order – to bring together curious juxtapositions. Items and events separated by time are forced to rub along together. But the Shaun Ryder index is so arch it is hard to resist the conclusion that there was a deliberate arrangement.

An index that mocks its subject isn't a new concept. The first example can be found at the back of Dr Bentley's *Dissertations on the Epistles of Phalaris, Examin'd* (1698), a takedown of the King's librarian. The authors used the index as a kind of hyper-abbreviated character assassination: 'his egregious dullness, p.74, 106, 119, 135, 136, 137, 241', 'his pedantry, from p.93 to 99, 144, 216' and 'his familiar acquaintance with books that he never saw, p.76, 98, 115, 232'.

The device caught on. In 1700, an anonymous pamphlet attacked the quackery that had begun to appear in the Royal Society's journal. Its snarky index directs readers to: 'Picking the Ears too much, Dangerous, p.15', and 'Mr Ray's definition of a Dildoe, p.11'.

In 1705, the Tory William Bromley ran for Speaker of the Commons. A decade earlier, Bromley had taken the Grand Tour and subsequently published his travel memoirs. Three days before the election, a new edition of Bromley's travelogue appeared, identical to the first but this time with an index.

The index singles out moments when Bromley is a little too familiar with Catholics ('The Author kiss'd the Pope's Slipper and had his Blessing, p.149') as well as plenty of examples of the young author stating the obvious or offering banalities: 'Parmesan Cheese from the dominions of Parma, p. 77', 'Pavements of Brick, or broad Stones, convenient for walking on, p. 68' and 'Eight Pictures take up less Room than Sixteen of the same Size, p. 14'.

Bromley lost the election and raged against the sneering index, assuming (correctly) that the anonymous author was the incumbent Speaker.

For the next decade or so, many other attack indexes pressed at the weak spots in their rivals' publications. A century later, the Whig historian Thomas Macaulay whispered a dying wish to his publisher: 'Let no damned Tory index my History!'

Indexes in today's celebrity memoirs are more whimsical than cruel. In the back pages of Joan Collins's *My Unapologetic Diaries*, my attention was drawn to 'Johnson, Boris, a vocal way with a kitchen implement, 281', and 'Prince Andrew, ducks a question about after-dark logistics, 231'. There is a knowingness at play that isn't quite serious and isn't quite Joan. These days I try not to judge books by their covers; I judge them by the index.

Index

abbeys 73
AC/DC 92
Albury 80
All England Club 17
Amis, Kingsley 89
Andersen, Hans Christian 90–1
Aristotle 101

Bagehot, Walter 39
bagpipes 60–1
Baker, Alice 27
Bank of England 72
Barnes, Julian 101
Bartlett, Frank 116
Bayley, Stephen 31, 79
Beach, Sylvia 71
Bean, Alan 92
Beauman, Francesca 124
Bell, Alexander Graham 92
Belmain, Steven 48
Bergius, Max 159
Big Ben 14–5
Birch, Dr Jonathan 146
Bobby, Brian 115
Bollinger the Bengal 154–5
Bonfire night 8
bossman 42
bowls 63
British Medical Journal 132–3
Brittain, Vera 173
Bromley, William 172
Brown, Zac 10
Burke, Edmund 39
Burlington Arcade 131
Burnham, Bo 10

Cain, Ethel Jane 115
Campeol, Ado 132
Campeol, Alba 132
canapés 42–3
Capstick, Ken 21
carp 12
cassoulet 81
Catholics 42
Chalke Valley History Festival 143
Charles II, King 28, 39

Charles III, King 39, 92
Chiswick Works 24–5
Christie, Agatha 80
cigarettes 164–5
Clement V, Pope 120
Clooney, George 149
cocaine 44–5
Cocker, Mark 141
Collins, Joan 125
Comisso, Giovanni 132
confetti 51
Conrad, Pete 92
Conran, Shirley 27
corks 22–3
Cranmer, Bishop 19
Crisp, Dave 126–7
croquet 17
Crystal Cruises 157

da Costa, Sara Mendes 115
Dali, Salvador 146–7
de Heem 146–7
de Nerval, Gérard 146
Denbies 80
Dicaeopolis 142
Dickens, Charles 51, 80
Domaine Gerovassiliou 23
doorstepping 84
Dorking 80
Drummond, Henry 80
Dubarry 99
Dungeons and Dragons 50

ecotypes 153
Ede, Jim 53
Edward VII, King 140
Eel's Footmen 16
elderflowers 58–9
Eliot, T.S. 98
Elizabeth I, Queen 116–7
Ellis, Clarence 52–3
Evelyn, John 80
evite 19

Ferretman 116
Forman, Lance 158–9

frankincense 96–7
French people 156

Garfield, James 92
Garsington Opera 105
gavage 36, 37
George III, King 80
gilets 54–5
'Gin Lane' 26
Go, Katy 79
Gore-Tex walkers 99
Guardian, the 101
guests 95
Guinness, Louise 109
Gunter, William 51

Hanzo, Hattori 171
Hardy, Thomas 99
Harrison, George 80
Hart, Charles 47
Hassell-McCosh,
 Jane 76–7
Hatshepsut 96
hawks 28
Hendrix, Jimi 69
Hepworth, Barbara 53
'Here Comes the Sun' 80
Herrick, Robert 35
herring 32–3
Hibernian Telegraph, the 124
Holroyd, Michael 53
Horsley, Sebastian 75
Huish Champflower 116–7
Hunter's Candy 9
Hutton, Ronald 150

jeans 10–1
Jerome, Jerome K. 50
Johnson, Boris 106
Johnson, Brian (AC/DC) 92
Johnson, Peter 22–3

Kawakami, Jinichi 171
Kennedy Jr, Robert F. 168
Kidston, Cath 78
Kill Bill 170

174

killer whales 152–3
Kim Jong-un 10
Kinnersley, Mr 39
Kipling, Rudyard 99, 164
Knights Templar 120
Kolb, William W. 9
Kriegsspiel 50

Land Rover Defender 13
'Lark Ascending, The' 80
Leakey, Dr Louis 80
Lilium longiflorum 40
Linguanotto, Roberto 132
Lucas, John 131

Macauley, Thomas 125
Magie, Elizabeth 65
Mangili, Enrico 51
Manners, Peverel 59
Martin, Tim 82–3
McCann, Peter 20
McCartney, Paul 149
McIlroy, Ed 168
merlins 28
moths 16
Mountford, Fiona 47
Muckle Flugga lighthouse 94
Mullins, William 80
Musashi, Miyamoto 171
myrrh 96–7

Naylor, Paul 38
Nibley, Hugh 51
Norman, Peter 92
Norse 62
North Korea 10

Olivier, Laurence 80
Orwell, George 33
Oughtred, William 80

pants 79
Paris 70–1
Parker Bros 65

Parsons, Nicholas 21
Phantom of the Opera, The 47
Philip IV, King 120
Philip, the Duke of
   Edinburgh, Prince 13
pigeons 102
Price, Jensen 12
Priestley, Rick 50
Prince of Wales pub 86–7
public hangings 167
pubs 66–7
pumpkins 150–1

Radecke, Marcus 78
Raleigh, Sir Walter 164
ready-to-drink cocktails
   26–7
restoration of Charles II 80
Richards, Keith 44
Rievaulx 73
Road to Wigan Pier, The 33
Robinson, Tom 69
Ronalde, Ronnie 131
Roy, Maj-Gen William 38
Ruane, Mandana 75
Ryder, Shaun 172
Ryland 73

St Agatha's Church 47
St-Martin-in-the-Fields 20
Sandyhills 93
Saturn 92
Scargill, Arthur 21
Schiaparelli, Elsa 146
Schmidt-Rubin rifle 163
Scholz, Olaf 113
Schweiger, Fräulein 47
Short, Doris 69
silver fox 149
Simmons, Pat 115
Snips McGee 146–7
Sole, Shaun 79
Sound of Music, The 47
Stendhal 156

Sutcliffe, Peter 20
Swiss Army 163–4

Taylor, Paul 134
Telegraph, the 76
Thatcher, Margaret 21, 33
throwing at cocks 166–7
Tiffany, Kaitlyn 129
Tiggy-Winkle, Mrs 141
Times, the 20, 36, 94, 172
Titchmarsh, Alan 10
toffee apple 42–3
trainers 30–1
Tsuruoka, Koji 77
Twitter 168

Uzeste 120–1

Vaughan, Adrian 68
Vaughan Williams, Ralph 80
Victorinox 162

Wace 118
wakizashi 171
Walker, Murray 21
Wallinger, Karl 20
Walton, Izaak 12
Warhammer 50
Warwick, Hugh 141
wassailing 34–5
Wells, H.G. 50
Wilmington, Earl of 92
Wimborne Militia 143
Wind in the Willows, The 72
Wodehouse, P.G. 80
Woodger, John 33
Wren, Christopher 80

X *see* Twitter

Yamada, Yuji 171

zebra danio 138–9
Zoological Gardens 138

175

Credits and Acknowledgements

We would like to thank *The Spectator*'s editor, Michael Gove, its publisher, Freddie Sayers, its managing editor Danielle Wall and our publisher at Quarto, Richard Green, all of whom jumped at the idea for this book with no hesitation and supported it through every stage. Thanks to every writer whose work features – it was a pleasure to reread and, in some cases, rediscover so many brilliant pieces.

We'd also like to thank Lukas Degutis for his help digging through picture archives, all *The Spectator*'s sub-editors for their diligence, Lara Prendergast, Mary Wakefield and Camilla Swift for commissioning and editing many excellent 'Notes on...' articles over the years, as well as the team at Quarto: Patrick Carpenter, Jennifer Barr, Chris Hancock and Rohana Yusof.

Lastly, special thanks must go to Michael Heath. Michael's first cartoon for *The Spectator* was published in 1957. Over nearly 70 years and under 15 editors, Michael's inimitable work has been integral to the spirit of the magazine. We are honoured that his cartoons illustrate this book.